WITHDRAWN

ABOUT THE AUTHOR

JAMES GOLDMAN has given us distinguished and successful work in a variety of fields. For the theater, he has written *The Lion in Winter; They Might Be Giants* (London); *Blood, Sweat and Stanley Poole* (with William Goldman); *Tolstoy* (London); *Follies* (with Stephen Sondheim); and the musical *A Family Affair*, for which he also wrote the lyrics with John Kander. His other lyrics include ballads for the films *Robin and Marian* and *The Lion in Winter*. For *The Lion in Winter*, he received an Academy Award and Best Screenplay awards from the Writers Guild of America and the Writers' Guild of Great Britain. His other films include *Nicholas and Alexandra, They Might Be Giants,* and *White Nights.* His novels are *Waldorf, The Man from Greek and Roman, Myself as Witness,* and *Fulton County.* For television, he has written *Evening Primrose* (with Stephen Sondheim), *Oliver Twist, Anna Karenina,* and the miniseries *Anastasia.* At the time of his death, in October 1998, Mr. Goldman had recently completed the book and lyrics for *The Celebrated, Scandalous, Heroic Misadventures of Tom Jones,* with music by Larry Grossman.

The LION in WINTER

The LION in WINTER

A Play

JAMES GOLDMAN

RANDOM HOUSE TRADE PAPERBACKS
New York

2004 Random House Trade Paperback Edition

Introduction copyright © 1981 by James Goldman
Copyright © 1966 by James Goldman
As an unpublished work copyright © 1964 by James Goldman

LIBRARY OF CONGRESS CATALOGING-IN-PUBLICATION DATA
Goldman, James. d. 1998
The lion in winter: a play / James Goldman.
p.   cm.
ISBN 0-8129-7335-6 (pbk.)
1. Henry II, King of England, 1133–1189—Drama.   2. Eleanor of
Aquitaine, Queen, consort of Henry II, King of England,
1122?–1204—Drama.   3. Great Britain—History—Henry II,
1154–1189—Drama.   4. Great Britain—Kings and rulers—Drama.
5. Marriages of royalty and nobility—Drama.
6. Queens—Great Britain—Drama.   I. Title.
PS3513.O337L5   2004
812'.54—dc22   2004050902

Random House website address: www.atrandom.com

Printed in the United States of America

2 4 6 8 9 7 5 3

For *BILL*

Most everyone who talks to me about *The Lion In Winter* is totally convinced the play has always been a great success. Even people who actually saw it during its run on Broadway are apt to mention what a hit it was or that they caught it in its second year. In point of fact, *Lion* opened on March 3, 1966 to highly contradictory notices, including a thunderous dismissal in the New York *Times*. Eighty-three performances later, it closed and sank from sight for what I was convinced would be forever.

Then came the film.

I still can't quite believe what happened. There are many plays that fail and then become successful movies; *Casablanca*, for example. But the play itself remains a failure; there were no new productions of *Everybody Came to Rick's*, the play on which the film was based. And there are other plays that attain a brief new lease on life from being filmed, only to disappear again. But *Lion*, as a stage piece was more than reprieved by the movie. It was transformed into a theater work that has been performed all over the world.

It still is, to this day. There are actually hundreds of stock and amateur productions every year. At this moment a ten-month tour mounted by the Long Wharf Theater is playing colleges and universities in thirty-odd states; a staging of it closed recently in Vienna, and another is to open shortly in Osaka, Japan.

Frankly, I'm amazed. I have no explanation why the play is still alive; or why it speaks as clearly as it does to younger audiences. There is, I know, a sense in which it is a family play; but this is hardly a unique distinction and I can't believe that it accounts for all this interest in the goings on at Chinon in 1183.

Whatever the explanation, I am eternally grateful. Not only for the obvious reasons, but for what it has meant to my life as a writer. I fell in love with the Plantagenets while writing *Lion* and I'm sure that, had the play stayed dead, I would never have gone back to them again.

I've done so twice thus far. Once in a film called *Robin and Marion*, in which King John appears; and, more recently, in *Myself As Witness*, a novel centered on the last years of John's life. I have no answer as to why it has been John who keeps recurring. Possibly because, of all the characters in *Lion*, he came off least well.

Not least well in the sense that he is poorly written, which, for all I know, is true enough, but rather in the way biographers must feel at having missed the shape or core or essence of their subject. Historians and storytellers don't have much in common, but they do share this: the past, once it gets hold of you, does actually come alive. For scholars, this is troublesome. For writers, it's the good stuff.

And improbable as it may sound, the people in the documents begin to breathe. They wriggle in your mind, they start to say things. Eleanor and Henry and their children sometimes seem as real to me as people I have dinner with. I feel as if I literally know them.

I have this feeling only now and then, I'm glad to say. I know that I have never met these characters. I made them up. I read about the things they did, I studied them and then imagined what they felt and thought and said and wanted from their lives. What they were really like, of course, no one will ever know. This is, I am convinced, a blessing, and I feel dismay for all the people who, a thousand years from now, will have our times on tape and film to study. They will see our faces, hear our voices, know it all and be deceived. They will be dealing with the surface, and the truth of things is always underneath. It has to be imagined.

So here are my imaginary king and queen and their imaginary children. I feel I know their faults, both as real people and as figures I've created, and I love them anyway. My one regret is that the play is written and I can't go back to the beginning and discover them again.

New York City

December, 1980

HISTORICAL NOTE

The historical material on Henry's reign is considerable inso-
far as battles, plots, wars, treaties and alliances are concerned. This play, while simplifying the political maneu-
vering—and combining a meeting of the French and English
Kings in 1183 with a Royal Court held at Windsor the following year into a Christmas Court that never was—is based
on the available data.

The facts we have, while clear enough as to the outcome
of relationships—such things as who kills whom and when
—say little if anything about the quality and content of those
relationships. The people in this play, their characters and
passions, while consistent with the facts we have, are fictions.

There were no laws of primogeniture in Henry's time. It
was a rare thing when the King was followed by his eldest
son. When kings died, it was open season on the English
throne, a fact responsible for much that Henry did.

THE LION IN WINTER *was first presented by Eugene V. Wolsk, Walter A. Hyman and Alan King with Emanuel Azenberg at the Ambassador Theatre in New York City on March 3, 1966, with the following cast:*

(In order of appearance)

HENRY II, King of England	Robert Preston
ALAIS CAPET	Suzanne Grossmann
JOHN	Bruce Scott
GEOFFREY	Dennis Cooney
RICHARD	James Rado
ELEANOR OF AQUITAINE	Rosemary Harris
PHILIP CAPET, King of France	Christopher Walken

Directed by Noel Willman

Scenery and costumes by Will Steven Armstrong

Lighting by Tharon Musser

Incidental music by Thomas Wagner

Production Manager: Jose Vega

SYNOPSIS OF SCENES

ACT ONE

SCENE 1: Alais's chamber, late afternoon.
SCENE 2: A Reception Hall, immediately following.
SCENE 3: Eleanor's chamber, some time later.
SCENE 4: The Reception Hall, immediately following.
SCENE 5: Eleanor's chamber, shortly afterwards.
SCENE 6: Philip's chamber, immediately following.

ACT TWO

SCENE 1: Henry's chamber, late at night.
SCENE 2: Alais's chamber, at dawn.
SCENE 3: The wine cellar, early morning.

The Time: Christmas, 1183.
The Place: Henry's palace at Chinon, France.
The Set: The palace at Chinon was famous for its grace and beauty. The arches, walls and columns of the set, though stone, are soft and light. There are no signs of royal wealth or pomp. The rooms in which the play occurs are simple, airy, clean and as free of furniture and things as possible.

The LION in WINTER

ACT ONE

ALAIS's *chamber. It is a small and graceful room, contain-*
ing just a bench, a chest and a chair. Late afternoon light
streams in through a window.

As the curtain rises, ALAIS CAPET, *dressed for a state occa-*
sion, is removing a small crown from her exquisite head. She
is twenty-three, serenely beautiful, and though glaring at
him at the moment, unmistakably in love with HENRY
PLANTAGENET. *He has just turned fifty, an age at which, in*
his time, men were either old or dead. Not HENRY. *Though*
arthritis comes occasionally and new battle wounds don't
heal the way the old ones did, he still is very nearly all he
ever was. He is enjoying that final rush of physical and men-
tal vigor that comes to some men not before the end but
just before the start of the decline. He wears, as always,
plain and unimpressive clothes.

As ALAIS *takes off her crown,* HENRY *turns to her and, with*
the beginnings of impatience, speaks.

HENRY   You must know that's a futile gesture. Come along.

ALAIS   No; I'll stay here and you can send reports.

HENRY   It's going to be a jungle of a day: if I start growling
now, I'll never last.

ALAIS   You'll last. You're like the rocks at Stonehenge; nothing knocks you down.

3

HENRY In these rooms, Alais, on this Christmas, I have all the enemies I need.

ALAIS You have more than you think.

HENRY Are you one? Has my willow turned to poison oak?

ALAIS If I decided to be trouble, Henry, how much trouble could I be?

HENRY Not much. You don't matter to the others; only me.

ALAIS How great a matter am I?

HENRY Alais, in my time I've known contessas, milkmaids, courtesans and novices, whores, gypsies, jades and little boys, but nowhere in God's Western world have I found anyone to love but you.

ALAIS And Rosamund.

HENRY She's dead.

ALAIS And Eleanor.

HENRY The new Medusa? My good wife?

ALAIS How is your Queen?

HENRY Decaying, I suppose.

ALAIS You haven't seen her?

HENRY No, nor smelled nor touched nor tasted. Don't be jealous of the gorgon; she is not among the things I love. How many husbands do you know who dungeon up their wives? I haven't kept the great bitch in the keep for ten years out of passionate attachment. Come. I've heard she's aging badly; let's go look.

ALAIS Would it be troublesome if I betrayed you?

HENRY We've no secrets, Eleanor and I. How can you possibly betray me?

ALAIS I could give away your plans.

HENRY You don't know what they are.

ALAIS I know you want to disinherit Richard.

HENRY So does Eleanor. She knows young Henry's dead. The Young King died in summer and I haven't named an heir. She knows I want John on the throne and I know she wants Richard. We are very frank about it.

ALAIS Henry, I can't be your mistress if I'm married to your son.

HENRY Why can't you? Johnny wouldn't mind.

ALAIS I do not like your Johnny.

HENRY He's a good boy.

ALAIS He's got pimples and he smells of compost.

HENRY He's just sixteen; he can't help the pimples.

ALAIS He could bathe.

HENRY It isn't such a dreadful thing to be a Queen of England. Not all eyes will weep for you.

ALAIS Will yours?

HENRY I don't know. Very likely.

ALAIS All I want is not to lose you. Can't you hide me? Can't I simply disappear?

HENRY You know you can't. Your little brother Philip's King of France now and he wants your wedding or your dowry back. I only took you for your dowry. You were seven. Two big knees and two big eyes and that's all. How was I to know?

ALAIS Let Philip have the dowry back. It isn't much.

HENRY I can't. The Vexin is a little county but it's vital to me.

ALAIS And I'm not.

HENRY It's been my luck to fall in love with landed women. When I married Eleanor, I thought: "You lucky man. The richest woman in the world. She owns the Aquitaine, the greatest province on the Continent—and beautiful as well." She was, you know.

ALAIS And you adored her.

HENRY Memory fails. There may have been an era when I did. (*Arranging a wisp of her hair*) Let's have one strand askew; nothing in life has any business being perfect.

ALAIS Henry, I was brought up to be dutiful. I smile a lot, bend easily and hope for very little. It is useful training and it's made a lot of hard things possible. But, Henry, not this thing.

HENRY I've had them summoned and I'll have you by me. With the headdress or without it.

ALAIS Oh, what difference does it make who's king?

HENRY What difference?

ALAIS Have you found religion, Henry? Are you going to look down from the clouds and see who's sitting in your place?

HENRY I've got to know before I die. I've built an empire and I've got to know it's going to last. I've put together England and I've added to it half of France. I am the greatest power in a thousand years. And after me comes John. If I can't leave this state to John, I've lived for nothing.

ALAIS John doesn't care for you at all.

HENRY We love each other deeply.

ALAIS None of them has any love for you.

HENRY Because we fight? Tell me they all three want the crown, I'll tell you it's a feeble prince that doesn't. They may snap at me or plot and that makes them the kind of sons I want. I've snapped and plotted all my life: there is no other way to be a king, alive and fifty all at once.

ALAIS I'm going to fight for you.

HENRY Oh, fine.

ALAIS When I was sixteen and we started this depraved relationship, I left everything to you. I lap sat, drank my milk and did what I was told. Not any more. Your cherub's twenty-three now and she's going to fight.

HENRY With mace and chain?

ALAIS With anything that I can think of.

HENRY That's exactly what I need: another mind at work. Try; you can hear the thinking through the walls. There's Geoffrey, humming treachery. And Richard, growling out for gore. And Eleanor, she's thinking heavy thoughts like molten lead and marble slabs. My house is full of intellectual activity.

ALAIS Add mine.

HENRY Alais, Alais—I don't plan to give you up. I don't plan to give up anything. I'll make alliances and bargains, threaten, beg, break heads and hearts, and when I'm done, I'll make an heir of John, a petty prince of Richard and I'll still have you.

ALAIS When can I believe you, Henry?

HENRY Always; even when I lie.

ALAIS How much is it safe to hope for?

HENRY Everything.

ALAIS But with so many enemies—

HENRY I know—and some of them are smarter folk than I or crueler or more ruthless or dishonest. But not all rolled in one. The priests write all the history these days and

7

they'll do me justice. Henry, they'll say, was a master bastard. (*Extending his arm*) Come; let's go downstairs and
meet the family.
　　　　(*She moves to join him*)

　　　　　　Dim and blackout

A Reception Hall, immediately following. It is a bright and spacious room. There is a bench, a large refectory table and a massive chair. A pile of holly boughs lies stacked in a corner.

*The young Plantagenets—*RICHARD, GEOFFREY *and* JOHN—*are entering as the lights rise.*

RICHARD LIONHEART, *at twenty-six, looks like his legend. He is handsome, graceful and impressive. He has been a famous soldier since his middle teens, and justly so; war is his profession and he is good at it.*

GEOFFREY, *Count of Brittany, is twenty-five. A man of energy and verve, he is attractive, charming and the owner of the best brain of a brainy family.*

JOHN, *at sixteen, does indeed have pimples. He is a charming-looking boy in spite of them, sweet-faced and totally adorable.*

They are bowing each other into the room when we see them.

JOHN   After you.

GEOFFREY   No; after you.

RICHARD   No; after you.

9

JOHN (*Delighted with himself as he skips into the room*) Oh, have it your way; after me.

RICHARD (*Following in, along with* GEOFFREY) You do keep growing, Johnny.

JOHN (*Agreeing cheerfully*) Every way but up. Look: holly. (*Beginning to hang the holly boughs*) I love Christmas.

GEOFFREY Warm and rosy time. The hot wine steams, the Yule log roars and we're the fat that's in the fire. She's here, you know.

JOHN Who?

RICHARD Mother.

GEOFFREY Since this morning.

RICHARD Have you seen her?

GEOFFREY Haven't you?

RICHARD We're not as friendly as we were.

GEOFFREY Does she still favor you?

RICHARD Does she or doesn't she?

JOHN If I'm supposed to make a fuss and kiss her hairy cheek, I won't.

RICHARD What you kiss, little prince, is up to you.

JOHN I'm Father's favorite; that's what counts.

RICHARD You hardly know me, Johnny, so I beg you to believe my reputation: I'm a constant soldier and a sometime poet and I will be king.

JOHN Just you remember: Father loves me best.

ELEANOR (*Sweeping in*) The way you bicker it's a wonder that he cares for any of you.

(ELEANOR OF AQUITAINE *is sixty-one and looks noth-*

*ing like it. She is a truly handsome woman of great
temperament, authority and presence. She has been a
queen of international importance for forty-six years
and you know it. Finally, she is that most unusual
thing: a genuinely feminine woman thoroughly ca-
pable of holding her own in a man's world)*

GEOFFREY   Mother.

ELEANOR   Geoffrey—but I do have handsome children. John
—you're so clean and neat. Henry takes good care of you.
And Richard. Don't look sullen, dear; it makes your eyes
go small and piggy and your chin look weak. Where's
Henry?

RICHARD   Upstairs with the family whore.

ELEANOR   That is a mean and tawdry way to talk about
your fiancée.

JOHN   My fiancée.

ELEANOR   Whosever fiancée, I brought her up and she is
dear to me and gentle. Have we seen the French King
yet?

GEOFFREY   Not yet.

ELEANOR   Let's hope he's grown up like his father—simon
pure and simon simple. Good, good Louis; if I'd managed
sons for him instead of all those little girls, I'd still be
stuck with being Queen of France and we should not
have known each other. Such, my angels, is the role of sex
in history. How's your father?

JOHN   Do you care?

ELEANOR   More deeply, lamb, than you can possibly imagine. Is my hair in place? I've given up the looking glass;
quicksilver has no sense of tact.

RICHARD   He still plans to make John king.

ELEANOR Of course he does. My, what a greedy little trinity you are: king, king, king. Two of you must learn to live with disappointment.

HENRY (*Entering, with* ALAIS) Ah—but which two?

ELEANOR Let's deny them all and live forever.

HENRY Tusk to tusk through all eternity. How was your crossing? Did the Channel part for you?

ELEANOR It went flat when I told it to; I didn't think to ask for more. How dear of you to let me out of jail.

HENRY It's only for the holidays.

ELEANOR Like school. You keep me young. Here's gentle Alais. (*As* ALAIS *starts to curtsy*) No, no; greet me like you used to. (*Hugging her*) Fragile I am not: affection is a pressure I can bear.

HENRY I've had the French King sent for. We will have a tactile conversation, like two surgeons looking for a lump. We'll state positions and I'll make the first of many offers. He'll refuse it, naturally, I'll make a better one and so on through the holidays until I win. For the duration of this joyous ritual, you will give, to your father, your support.

RICHARD Why will I?

ELEANOR Out of duty, dear. (*To* HENRY) Tell me, what's Philip like? I hear he's quite impressive for a boy of seventeen—

HENRY (*As* PHILIP *enters*) My Lord.

ELEANOR Oh—and you are. I'm Eleanor, who might have been your mother. All the others here you know.

PHILIP (PHILIP CAPET *is indeed impressive. He is tall, well-proportioned and handsome without being at all pretty. His manner is open, direct and simple and he smiles easily. He has been King of France for three years and has learned a great deal. He bows)* Queen Eleanor—Your Grace.

HENRY My Lord. Welcome to Chinon.

PHILIP Sir.

HENRY Your grievances, as we have understood them, have to do with Princess Alais and her dowry.

PHILIP Sixteen years ago you made a treaty with us. It is time its terms were executed.

HENRY We are willing to discuss it.

PHILIP Our position comes to this: that you will either hold the marriage or return the Vexin. Alais marries Richard or we'll have the county back at once.

HENRY That's clear, concise and well presented. My position is—Well, frankly, Philip, it's a tangle. Once I'm dead, who's to be king? I could draw papers till my scribes drop or the ink runs out and once I died, unless I've left behind me three contented sons, my lands will split three ways in civil war. You see my problem?

PHILIP Clearly; but it's yours, not mine.

HENRY Two years ago the Queen and I, for reasons passing understanding, gave the Aquitaine to Richard. That makes Richard very powerful. How can I give him Alais, too? The man she marries has you for an ally.

PHILIP It's their wedding or the Vexin back. Those are the terms you made with Louis.

HENRY True but academic, lad. The Vexin's mine.

PHILIP By what authority?

HENRY It's got my troops all over it: that makes it mine. Now hear me, boy. You take what memories you have of me and mark them out of date. I'm not your father's friend, now; I'm his son's opponent.

PHILIP I'm a king: I'm no man's boy.

HENRY A king? Because you put your ass on purple cush-
ions?

PHILIP Sir.
    (*He turns on his heel and starts to go*)

HENRY Philip, you haven't got the feel of this at all. Use all
your voices: when I bellow, bellow back.

PHILIP I'll mark that down.

HENRY This, too. We are the world in small. A nation is a
human thing; it does what we do, for our reasons. Surely,
if we're civilized, it must be possible to put the knives
away. We can make peace. We have it in our hands.

PHILIP I've tutors of my own. Will that be all?

HENRY Oh, think. You came here for a reason. You've
made demands of me. Now don't you want to ask me if
I've got an offer?

PHILIP Have you got an offer?

HENRY Not yet—but I'll think of one. (PHILIP *starts off
again*) Oh, by the way . . . (*At the doorway,* PHILIP
turns) You're better at this than I thought you'd be.

PHILIP (*Smiling*) I wasn't sure you'd noticed.
    (*He exits*)

HENRY Well—what shall we hang? The holly or each
other?

ELEANOR You can't read your sons at all. That isn't anger
they're projecting; it's anxiety.

HENRY I read them. I know Richard's moods and Johnny's
faces and the thought behind the pitch of Geoffrey's
voice. The trouble's at the other end; they don't know me.
(*Turning to his sons*) There is a legend of a king called
Lear with whom I have a lot in common. Both of us have

kingdoms and three children we adore and both of us are old. But there it stops. He cut his kingdom into bits. I can't do that. I've built this house and it will stand. What I have architected, you will not destroy.

RICHARD Would you say, Father, that I have the makings of a king?

HENRY A splendid king.

RICHARD Would you expect me, Father, to be disinherited without a fight?

HENRY Of course you'll fight. I raised you to.

RICHARD I don't care what you offer Philip. I don't care what plans you make. I'll have the Aquitaine and Alais and the crown. I'll have them all.

JOHN You're going to love my coronation.

RICHARD I won't give up one to get the other. I won't trade off Alais or the Aquitaine to this (*Indicating* JOHN)—this walking pustule. No, your loving son will not.
    (*He exits*)

JOHN Did you hear what he called me?

ELEANOR Clearly, dear. Now run along; it's nearly dinner-time.

JOHN I only do what Father tells me.

HENRY Go and eat.

JOHN Did I say something wrong? I'm always saying something wrong. All right, I'll eat, I'll eat.
    (*He exits*)

ELEANOR And that's to be the king.

GEOFFREY And I'm to be his chancellor. Has he told you? John will rule the country while I run it. That's to say, he gets to spend the taxes that I get to raise.

ELEANOR   How nice for you.

GEOFFREY   It's not as nice as being king.

HENRY   We've made you Duke of Brittany. Is that so little?

GEOFFREY   No one ever thinks of crowns and mentions Geoff. Why is that? I make out three prizes here—a throne, a princess and the Aquitaine. Three prizes and three sons; but no one ever says, "Here, Geoff, here Geoff boy, here's a bone for you."

HENRY   I should have thought that being chancellor was a satisfying bone.

GEOFFREY   It isn't power that I feel deprived of; it's the mention that I miss. There's no affection for me here. You wouldn't think I'd want that, would you?
    (*He exits*)

ELEANOR   Henry, I have a confession.

HENRY   Yes?

ELEANOR   I don't much like our children. (*To* ALAIS) Only you—the child I raised but didn't bear.

ALAIS   You never cared for me.

ELEANOR   I did and do. Believe me, Henry's bed is Henry's province: he can people it with sheep for all I care. Which, on occasion, he has done.

HENRY   Still that? When Rosamund's been dead for seven years?

ELEANOR   Two months and eighteen days. I never liked her much.

HENRY   You count the days?

ELEANOR   I made the numbers up. (*To* ALAIS) He found Miss Clifford in the mists of Wales and brought her home for closer observation. Liking what he saw, he scrutinized her many years. He loved her deeply and she him. And yet, my dear, when Henry had to choose between his lady and my lands—

ALAIS   He'll leave me if he has to; I know that.

ELEANOR   Poor Alais.

ALAIS   There's no sport in hurting me; it is so easy.

ELEANOR   After all the years of love, the hair I've brushed and braided and the tears I've kissed away, do you think I could bring myself to hurt you?

ALAIS   Eleanor, with both hands tied behind you.
   (*She exits*)

HENRY   She is lovely, isn't she?

ELEANOR   Yes, very.

HENRY   If I'd chosen, who could I have picked to love to gall you more?

ELEANOR   There's no one. (*Moving to the holly boughs*) Come on; let's finish Christmasing the place.

HENRY   Time hasn't done a thing but wrinkle you.

ELEANOR   It hasn't even done that. I have borne six girls, five boys and thirty-one connubial years of you. How am I possible?

HENRY   (*Joining her in hanging holly*) There are moments when I miss you.

ELEANOR   Many?

HENRY   Do you doubt it?

ELEANOR   (*Rumpling his hair*) That's my woolly sheep dog. So wee Johnny gets the crown.

HENRY   I've heard it rumored but I don't believe it.

ELEANOR   Losing Alais will be hard, for you do love her.

HENRY It's an old man's last attachment; nothing more. How hard do you find living in your castle?

ELEANOR It was difficult in the beginning but that's past. I find I've seen the world enough. I have my maids and menials in my courtyard and I hold my little court. It suits me now.

HENRY I'll never let you loose. You led too many civil wars against me.

ELEANOR And I damn near won the last one. Still, as long as I get trotted out for Christmas Courts and state occasions now and then—for I do like to see you—it's enough. Do you still need the Vexin, Henry?

HENRY Need you ask?

ELEANOR My strategy is ten years old.

HENRY It is as crucial as it ever was. My troops there are a day away from Paris, just a march of twenty miles. I must keep it.

ELEANOR (*Surveying the holly*) I'd say that's all the jollying this room can stand. I'm famished. Let's go in to dinner.

HENRY (*Extending his arm*) Arm in arm.

ELEANOR (*Taking his arm and smiling at him*) And hand in hand. You're still a marvel of a man.

HENRY And you're my lady.

ELEANOR Henry, dear, if Alais doesn't marry Richard, I will see you lose the Vexin.

HENRY Well, I thought you'd never say it.

ELEANOR I can do it.

HENRY You can try.

ELEANOR My Richard is the next king, not your John. I

know you, Henry. I know every twist and bend you've got and I'll be waiting round each corner for you.

HENRY   Do you truly care who's king?

ELEANOR   I care because you care so much.

HENRY   I might surprise you. Eleanor, I've fought and bargained all these years as if the only thing I lived for was what happened after I was dead. I've something else to live for now. I've blundered onto peace.

ELEANOR   On Christmas Eve.

HENRY   Since Louis died, while Philip grew, I've had no France to fight. And in that lull, I've found how good it is to write a law or make a tax more fair or sit in judgment to decide which peasant gets a cow. There is, I tell you, nothing more important in the world. And now the French boy's big enough and I am sick of war.

ELEANOR   Come to your question, Henry; make the plea. What would you have me do? Give out, give up, give in?

HENRY   Give me a little peace.

ELEANOR   A little? Why so modest? How about eternal peace? Now there's a thought.

HENRY   If you oppose me, I will strike you any way I can.

ELEANOR   Of course you will.

HENRY   (*Taking her arm as before*)   We have a hundred barons we should look the loving couple for.

ELEANOR   (*Smiling at him*)   Can you read love in that?

HENRY   And permanent affection.

ELEANOR   (*As they start, grand and stately, for the wings*)   Henry?

HENRY   Madam?

ELEANOR   Did you ever love me?

HENRY   No.

ELEANOR   Good. That will make this pleasanter.

Dim and blackout

ELEANOR'S *chamber, some time later. A plain and pleasant room, it holds a chair, a table and a low wood chest. Soft tapestries give warmth and color. As the lights rise,* ELEANOR *is seated at the table wrapping Christmas presents. She looks up as* RICHARD *appears.*

RICHARD   All right. I've come. I'm here. What was it you wanted?

ELEANOR   Just to talk. We haven't been alone, the two of us, in—How long is it, lamb? Two years? You look fit. War agrees with you. I keep informed. I follow all your slaughters from a distance. Do sit down.

RICHARD   Is this an audience, a goodnight kiss with cookies or an ambush?

ELEANOR   Let us hope it's a reunion. Must you look so stern? I sent for you to say I want your love again but I can't say it to a face like that.

RICHARD   My love, of all things. What could you want it for?

ELEANOR   Why, for itself. What other purpose could I have?

RICHARD   You'll tell me when you're ready to.

ELEANOR   I scheme a lot; I know. I plot and plan. That's

21

how a queen in prison spends her time. But there is more to me than that. My mind's not disembodied. Can't I say I love a son and be believed?

RICHARD   If I were you, I'd try another tack. I have no dammed-up floods of passion for you. There's no chance I'll overflow.

ELEANOR   You are a dull boy.

RICHARD   Am I?

ELEANOR   Dull as plainsong: la, la, la, forever on one note. I gave the Church up out of boredom. I can do as much for you.

RICHARD   You'll never give me up; not while I hold the Aquitaine.

ELEANOR   You think I'm motivated by a love of real estate?

RICHARD   I think you want it back. You're so deceitful you can't ask for water when you're thirsty. We could tangle spiders in the webs you weave.

ELEANOR   If I'm so devious, why don't you go? Don't stand there quivering in limbo. Love me, little lamb, or leave me.

RICHARD   (*Not moving*) Leave you, madam? With pure joy.

ELEANOR   Departure is a simple act. You put the left foot down and then the right.

JOHN   (*Entering, in high spirits, followed by* GEOFFREY) Mother—

ELEANOR   Hush, dear. Mother's fighting.

JOHN   Father's coming with the treaty terms.

ELEANOR   No doubt he's told you what they are.

22

JOHN   He doesn't have to. Don't you think I know which end is up?

ELEANOR   Of course you do, dear. Has he put the terms to Philip?

HENRY   (*Entering, with* ALAIS)   Not yet, but we're shortly granting him an audience. I hope you'll all attend.

ELEANOR   Are we to know the terms or have you come to tease us?

HENRY   Not at all. The terms are these.

RICHARD   What are you giving up to Philip? What of mine?

JOHN   Whatever you've got goes to me.

GEOFFREY   And what's the nothing Geoffrey gets?

HENRY   For God's sake, boys, you can't all three be king.

RICHARD   All three of us can try.

HENRY   That's pointless now. The treaty calls for you to marry Alais and you shall. I want you to succeed me, Richard. Alais and the crown: I give you both.

RICHARD   I've got no sense of humor. If I did, I'd laugh.

HENRY   I've used you badly, haven't I?

RICHARD   You've used me cleverly and well.

HENRY   Not any more. I mean to do it.

JOHN   What about me? I'm your favorite, I'm the one you love.

HENRY   John, I can't help myself. Stand next to Richard. See how you compare. Could you keep anything I gave you? Could you beat him on the field?

JOHN   You could.

HENRY   But, John, I won't be there.

JOHN Let's fight him now.

HENRY How can I? There's no way to win. I'm losing too, John. All my dreams for you are lost.

JOHN You've led me on.

HENRY I never meant to.

JOHN You're a failure as a father, you know that.

HENRY I'm sorry, John.

JOHN Not yet you're not. But I'll do something terrible and you'll be sorry then.

ELEANOR Did you rehearse all this or are you improvising?

HENRY Good God, woman, face the facts.

ELEANOR Which ones? We've got so many.

HENRY Power is the only fact. (*Indicating* RICHARD) He is our ablest son. He is the strongest, isn't he? How can I keep him from the crown? He'd only take it if I didn't give it to him.

RICHARD No—you'd make me fight to get it. I know you: you'd never give me everything.

HENRY True—and I haven't. You get Alais and you get the kingdom but I get the one thing I want most. If you're king, England stays intact. I get that. It's all yours now— the girl, the crown, the whole black bloody business. Isn't that enough?
  (*He exits*)

ALAIS I don't know who's to be congratulated. Not me, certainly. (*To* ELEANOR) You got me for your Richard. How'd you manage it? Did you tell him he's your woolly lamb? Or say how much you like it in your castle?

ELEANOR It's all lies but I told him.

ALAIS Kings, queens, knights everywhere you look and I'm
the only pawn. I haven't got a thing to lose: that makes
me dangerous.
(*She exits*)

ELEANOR Poor child.

JOHN Poor John—who says poor John? Don't everybody
sob at once. My God, if I went up in flames, there's not a
living soul who'd pee on me to put the fire out.

RICHARD Let's strike a flint and see.

JOHN He hates me. Why? What should he hate me for?
Am I the eldest son? Am I the heir? Am I the hero?
What's my crime? Is it some childhood score, some baby
hurt? When I was six and you were sixteen, did I brutal-
ize you? What?

ELEANOR For whatever I have done to you, forgive me.

JOHN What could you have done? You were never close
enough.

ELEANOR When you were little, you were torn from me:
blame Henry.

JOHN I was torn from you by midwives and I haven't seen
you since.

ELEANOR Then blame me if it helps.

RICHARD No, it's the midwives' fault. They threw the baby
out and kept the afterbirth.

JOHN You're everything a little brother dreams of. You
know that? I used to dream about you all the time.

ELEANOR Oh, Johnny . . .

JOHN That's right, Mother; mother me.

ELEANOR Yes, if you'd let me.

JOHN Let you? Let you put your arms around me just the

25

way you never did? (*They are close*) You can do it. Think I'm Richard. (*She puts her arms around him*) That's it. That's the way. Now kiss my scabby cheek and run your fingers through my hair.

ELEANOR John, John . . .

JOHN (*Wrenching away*) No—it's all false. You know what I am? I'm the family nothing. Geoffrey's smart and Richard's brave and I'm not anything.

ELEANOR You are to me.

JOHN I'll show you, Eleanor. I haven't lost yet. (*Moving to go*) Geoff.

GEOFFREY In a minute.

JOHN What's that?

GEOFFREY Run along. I'm busy now.

JOHN I give the orders. I'm the master. When I call, you come.

GEOFFREY There's news in Chinon, John. That falling sound was you.

JOHN The woods are full of chancellors.

GEOFFREY And the castle's full of kings.

JOHN Oh, you're not really leaving me?

GEOFFREY No; I've already left.

JOHN I don't care. I don't need anybody.
(*He exits*)

GEOFFREY Well, Mummy, here I am.

ELEANOR John's lost a chancellor, has he?

GEOFFREY And you've gained one.

ELEANOR It's a bitter thing your Mummy has to say.

GEOFFREY She doesn't trust me.

ELEANOR You must know Henry isn't through with John. He'll keep the Vexin till the moon goes blue from cold and as for Richard's wedding day, we'll see the second coming first; the needlework alone can last for years.

GEOFFREY I know. You know I know. I know you know I know, we know that Henry knows and Henry knows we know it. We're a knowledgeable family. Do you want my services or don't you?

ELEANOR Why are you dropping John?

GEOFFREY Because you're going to win.

ELEANOR I haven't yet.

GEOFFREY You will with me to help you. I can handle John. He'll swallow anything I tell him and I'll take him by the hand and walk him into any trap you set.

ELEANOR You're good, you're first class, Geoff. Did John agree?

GEOFFREY To what?

ELEANOR To making you his chancellor for betraying me?

GEOFFREY I have some principles.

ELEANOR Then how much did you get from Henry?

GEOFFREY Get from Henry?

ELEANOR What's the fee for selling me to him? Or have you found some way of selling everyone to everybody?

GEOFFREY Not yet, Mummy, but I'm working on it. I don't care who's king but you and Henry do. I want to watch the two of you go picnicking on one another.

ELEANOR Yes, it's true; you really mean it.

GEOFFREY Do you blame me?

ELEANOR   You've a gift for hating.

GEOFFREY   You're the expert; you should know.

ELEANOR   You've loved me all these years.

GEOFFREY   Well, God forgive me, I've upset the Queen. Madam, may you rot.

ELEANOR   We need you. Help us.

GEOFFREY   What? And miss the fun of selling you?

ELEANOR   Be Richard's chancellor.

GEOFFREY   Rot.
            (*He exits*)

ELEANOR   Oh, Geoffrey. Well, that's how deals are made. We've got him if we want him. I should like some wine. Why did I have to have such clever children? He will sell us all, you know; but only if he thinks we think he won't. Scenes. I can't touch my sons except in scenes. (RICHARD *gives her a glass of wine*) What's the matter, Richard?

RICHARD   Nothing.

ELEANOR   It's a heavy thing, your nothing. When I write or send for you or speak or reach, your nothings come. Like stones.

RICHARD   Don't play a scene with me.

ELEANOR   I wouldn't if I could.

RICHARD   There'd be no profit in it. That's my one advantage over you. You're wiser, shrewder, more experienced. I'm colder; I feel less.

ELEANOR   Why, you don't know yourself at all. I've known who I am some years now. I had, at one time, many appetites. I wanted poetry and power and the young men who create them both. I even wanted Henry, too, in those days. Now I've only one desire left: to see you king.

RICHARD   The only thing you want to see is Father's vitals
on a bed of lettuce. You don't care who wins as long as
Henry loses. You'd see Philip on the throne. You'd feed us
to the Franks or hand us to the Holy Romans. You'd do
anything.

ELEANOR   (*Nodding wearily*)   That's good to know.

RICHARD   You are Medea to the teeth but this is one son
you won't use for vengeance on your husband.

ELEANOR   I could bend you. I could wear you like a brace-
let—but I'd sooner die.

RICHARD   You're old enough to die, in any case.

ELEANOR   How my captivity has changed you. Henry
meant to hurt me and he's hacked you up instead. More
wine. (*He takes the glass and goes to pour. She gazes at
the hand that held the glass*) Men coveted this talon
once. Henry was eighteen when we met and I was Queen
of France. He came down from the North to Paris with a
mind like Aristotle's and a form like mortal sin. We shattered the Commandments on the spot. I spent three
months annulling Louis and in spring, in May not far
from here, we married. Young Count Henry and his
Countess. But in three years' time, I was his Queen and
he was King of England. Done at twenty-one. Five years
your junior, General.

RICHARD   I can count.

ELEANOR   No doubt the picture of your parents being fond
does not hang in your gallery—but we were fond. There
was no Thomas Becket then, or Rosamund. No rivals—
only me. And then young Henry came and you and all
the other blossoms in my garden. Yes, if I'd been sterile,
darling, I'd be happier today.

RICHARD   Is that designed to hurt me?

ELEANOR   What a waste. I've fought with Henry over who

comes next, whose dawn is it and which son gets the sunset and we'll never live to see it. Look at you. I loved you more than Henry and it's cost me everything.

RICHARD What do you want?

ELEANOR I want us back the way we were.

RICHARD That's not it.

ELEANOR All right, then. I want the Aquitaine.

RICHARD Now that's the mother I remember.

ELEANOR No, it's not at all, but if you find her more congenial, she's the one you'll get. We can win. I can get you Alais. I can make the marriage happen—but I've got to have the Aquitaine to do it. I must have it back.

RICHARD You were better in your scene with Geoffrey.

ELEANOR Shall I write my will? "To Richard, everything." Would you believe me then? Where's paper?

RICHARD Paper burns.

ELEANOR And tears and turns to pudding in the rain. What can I do?

RICHARD I did think Geoffrey put it nicely. You can rot.

ELEANOR I love you.

RICHARD You love nothing. You are incomplete. The human parts of you are missing. You're as dead as you are deadly.

ELEANOR Don't leave me.

RICHARD You were lovely once. I've seen the pictures.

ELEANOR Oh, don't you remember how you loved me?

RICHARD Vaguely—like a legend.

ELEANOR You remember. We were always hand in hand. (*Thrusting her hand in his*) That's how it felt.

RICHARD As coarse and hot as that.

ELEANOR (*Snatching her hand away*) This won't burn. I'll scratch a will on this. (*Baring her forearm, with a small knife suddenly in her other hand*) To Richard, everything.

RICHARD (*As she draws the blade across the flesh*) Mother!

ELEANOR Remember how I taught you numbers and the lute and poetry.

RICHARD (*As they hold each other*) Mother.

ELEANOR See? You do remember. I taught you dancing, too, and languages and all the music that I knew and how to love what's beautiful. The sun was warmer then and we were every day together.

Dim and blackout

The Reception Hall, immediately following. A Christmas tree has been added to the room. JOHN *is drinking from a bottle as the lights rise.* GEOFFREY *enters, calling.*

GEOFFREY   John—there you are.

JOHN   Go find yourself another fool.

GEOFFREY   You're angry: good. Now, here's my plan.

JOHN   You are a rancid bastard. Want to fight?

GEOFFREY   John, use your head. Would I betray you?

JOHN   Why not? Everybody else does.

GEOFFREY   John, I only turned on you to get their confidence. It worked; they trust me.

JOHN   I tell you, your leg could fall off at the pelvis and I wouldn't trust the stump to bleed.

GEOFFREY   If you're not king, I'm nothing. You're my way to power, John.

JOHN   I still don't trust you.

GEOFFREY   Always put your faith in vices. Trust my slyness if you think I'm sly. Make use of me, deceive me, cast me off—but not until I've made you king.

JOHN   You think I can't out-think you, do you? All right, what's your plan?

GEOFFREY   We've got to make a deal with Philip.

JOHN   Why?

GEOFFREY   Because you're out and Richard's in.

JOHN   What kind of deal?

GEOFFREY   A war. If we three join and fight now, we can finish Richard off.

JOHN   You mean destroy him?

GEOFFREY   Yes.

JOHN   And Mother, too?

GEOFFREY   And Mother, too. Well, do we do it? Is it on?

JOHN   I've got to think.

GEOFFREY   We're extra princes now. You know where extra princes go.

JOHN   Down?

GEOFFREY   Very down.

PHILIP   (*Entering*)   I see I'm early for my audience. Or am I late?

GEOFFREY   No, you're exquisitely on time. I feel the strangest sense of kinship with you, Philip.

PHILIP   So you've sensed it, too.

GEOFFREY   How far around the corner were you?

PHILIP   How'd you know?

GEOFFREY   You came in so conveniently.

PHILIP   I'll learn.

GEOFFREY   Well, was there anything you didn't overhear?

PHILIP   John's answer. Does he want a war or doesn't he?

34

THE LION IN WINTER

GEOFFREY   Do you? If John asks for your soldiers, will he get them?

PHILIP   If John wants a war, he's got one.

GEOFFREY   John, you hear that?

JOHN   I'm still thinking.

GEOFFREY   Let me help. It's either Richard on the throne or you.

JOHN (*To* PHILIP)   You think we'd win?

PHILIP   I know it.

JOHN   Father's coming.

GEOFFREY (*Moving to exit*)   This way. We've got plans to make. (*Turning back as* PHILIP *exits*) John.

JOHN   In a minute.
      (GEOFFREY *exits*)

HENRY (*Entering with* ALAIS. *To* ALAIS)   I'd appreciate a little quiet confidence. I have enough nits picking at me.

JOHN   Father, have you got a minute?

HENRY   What for?

JOHN   If you had a minute, we could talk.

HENRY   I'm busy now. Have you seen Philip?

JOHN   Look: you know that hunting trip we're taking on my birthday?

HENRY   Well?

JOHN   Forget it. I'm not going.

HENRY   Why not?

JOHN   I'm just not.

HENRY   But, John, the trip's all planned.

35

JOHN (*Moving to go*) I'll go get Philip for you.

HENRY You did have a good time last year, didn't you?

JOHN I loved it.

HENRY What's wrong, lad?

JOHN You're busy.

HENRY True enough but—

JOHN You've got more important things to do.

HENRY I can't make things all right if I don't know what's wrong.

JOHN You're giving Richard everything.

HENRY You think I'd do that?

JOHN You don't love me any more.

HENRY Don't pout—and stand up straight. How often do I have to tell you?

JOHN When's my coronation?

HENRY When I say so.

JOHN That's no answer.
(*He starts off*)

HENRY John.

JOHN Tell her how much you love her. You're a wonder with the women.
(*He exits*)

HENRY What in hell was that about?

ALAIS He heard you disinherit him upstairs and wondered if you meant it.

HENRY If I meant it? When I've fathered him and mothered him and babied him? He's all I've got. How often does he have to hear it? Every supper? Should we start the soup with who we love and who we don't?

ALAIS I heard you promise me to Richard.

HENRY You don't think I meant it?

ALAIS I think you enjoy it, passing me from hand to hand. What am I to you—a collection plate? Or am I all you've got, like John?

HENRY I've got to get the Aquitaine for John.

ALAIS I talk people and you answer back in provinces.

HENRY They get mixed up. What's the Aquitaine to Eleanor? It's not a province, it's a way to torture me. That's why she's upstairs wooing Richard, wheezing on the coals. She'll squeeze it out of him. God, but I'd love to eavesdrop. (*Doing* ELEANOR) I taught you prancing, lamb, and lute and flute—

ELEANOR (*Entering, carrying a great pile of Christmas boxes*) That's marvelous; it's absolutely me. (*He takes some from her*) There you are. I thought as long as I was coming down I'd bring them. Where's the tree?

HENRY (*Leading the way to it*) Whatever are you giving me?

ELEANOR You're such a child: you always ask.

HENRY (*Reading from a package*) To Henry. (*Weighing it*) Heavy. (*Delighted*) It's my headstone. Eleanor, you spoil me.

ELEANOR I never could deny you anything.

ALAIS You've grown old gracefully, you two; I'll give you that.

HENRY (*As* ALAIS *starts to go*) Don't go. It nettles her to see how much I need you.

ALAIS You need me, Henry, like a tailor needs a tinker's dam.

HENRY Alais—

ALAIS I know that look. He's going to say he loves me.

HENRY Like my life. (*She turns sharply and exits*) I talk like that to keep her spirits up. Well, how'd you do with Richard? Did you break his heart?

ELEANOR You think he ought to give me back the Aquitaine?

HENRY I can't think why he shouldn't. After all, I've promised him the throne.

ELEANOR The boy keeps wondering if your promises are any good.

HENRY There's no sense asking if the air's good when there's nothing else to breathe.

ELEANOR Exactly what I told him.

HENRY Have you got it? Will he give it back?

ELEANOR How can you think I'd ever pass it on to John?

HENRY It matters to me desperately.

ELEANOR Why should it? Does it matter what comes after us?

HENRY Ask any sculptor, ask Praxiteles, "Why don't you work in butter?" Eleanor, because it doesn't last.

ELEANOR Is Johnny bronze? He'll go as green from mold as any of our sons.

HENRY I know that. Richard gets the throne. You heard my promise. What else do you want?

ELEANOR No Aquitaine for John.

38

HENRY I've got to give him something. Isn't some agreement possible?

ELEANOR Love, in a world where carpenters get resurrected, anything is possible.

HENRY You bore him, dammit; he's your son.

ELEANOR Oh, heavens yes. Two hundred eighty days I bore him. I recall them all. You'd only just found Rosamund.

HENRY Why her so damn particularly? I've found other women.

ELEANOR Countless others.

HENRY What's your count? Let's have a tally of the bedspreads you've spread out on.

ELEANOR Thomas Becket's.

HENRY That's a lie.

ELEANOR I know it. Jealousy looks silly on us, Henry.

HENRY Doesn't it.

ELEANOR You still care what I do.

HENRY I want the Aquitaine for John. I want it and I'll have it.

ELEANOR Is that menace you're conveying? Is it to be torture? Will you boil me or stretch me, which? Or am I to be perforated?

HENRY I have the documents and you will sign.

ELEANOR How can you force me to? Threats? Sign or I refuse to feed you? Tears? Oh, sign before my heart goes crack. Bribes, offers, deals? I'm like the earth, old man; there isn't any way around me.

HENRY I adore you.

ELEANOR Save your aching arches; that road is closed.

HENRY I've got an offer for you, *ma jolie*.

ELEANOR A deal, a deal. I give the richest province on the Continent to John for what? You tell me, mastermind. For what?

HENRY Your freedom.

ELEANOR Oh.

HENRY Once Johnny has the Aquitaine, you're free. I'll let you out. Think: on the loose in London, winters in Provence, impromptu trips to visit Richard anywhere he's killing people. All that for a signature.

ELEANOR You're good.

HENRY I thought it might appeal to you. You always fancied traveling.

ELEANOR Yes, I did. I even made poor Louis take me on Crusade. How's that for blasphemy? I dressed my maids as Amazons and rode bare-breasted halfway to Damascus. Louis had a seizure and I damn near died of windburn but the troops were dazzled. Henry, I'm against the wall.

HENRY Because I've put you there, don't think I like to see it.

ELEANOR I believe it; you do feel for me. To be a prisoner, to be bricked in when you've known the world—I'll never know how I've survived. These ten years, Henry, have been unimaginable. And you can offer me the only thing I want if I give up the only thing I treasure and still feel for me. You give your falcons more affection than I get.

HENRY My falcons treat me better.

ELEANOR Handle me with iron gloves, then.

HENRY Sign the papers and we'll break the happy news.

The Queen is free, John joins the landed gentry, Philip's satisfied and Richard gets a princess.

ELEANOR Yes. Let's have it done. I'll sign. On one condition.

HENRY Name it.

ELEANOR Have the wedding now.

HENRY What's that?

ELEANOR Why, I've surprised you. Surely it's not sudden. They've been marching down the aisle for sixteen years and that's a long walk. John can be the best man—that's a laugh—and you can give the bride away. I want to watch you do it.

HENRY Alais—I can live without her.

ELEANOR And I thought you loved her.

HENRY So I do.

ELEANOR Thank God. You frightened me: I was afraid this wouldn't hurt.

HENRY You fill me full of fear and pity. What a tragedy you are.

ELEANOR I wonder, do you ever wonder if I slept with Geoffrey?

HENRY With my father?

ELEANOR It's not true but one hears rumors. Don't you ever wonder?

HENRY Is it rich, despising me? Is it rewarding?

ELEANOR No—it's terrible.

HENRY Then stop it.

ELEANOR How? It's what I live for.

HENRY   Rosamund, I loved you!

ELEANOR (*Calling*)   John—Richard—Geoffrey.

HENRY   Where's a priest? I'll do it. I'll show you. By Christ, I will. (*As* PHILIP, JOHN *and* GEOFFREY *enter from one side,* ALAIS *and* RICHARD *come in from the other*) Somebody dig me up a priest.

JOHN   What for? What's happened?

ELEANOR   Richard's getting married.

JOHN   Now? He's getting married now?

ELEANOR   I never cease to marvel at the quickness of your mind.

JOHN   You can't hurt me, you bag of bile, no matter what you say. (*To* HENRY) But you can. Father, why?

HENRY   Because I say so. (*To* GEOFFREY) You. Bring me a bishop.

ELEANOR (*As* GEOFFREY *starts to go*)   Get old Durham. He's just down the hall. (GEOFFREY *exits. To* ALAIS) You'll make a lovely bride. I wonder if I'll cry.

ALAIS   You sound as if you think it's going to happen.

ELEANOR   And I do.

ALAIS   He's only plotting. Can't you tell when Henry's plotting?

ELEANOR   Not this time.

ALAIS   He'll never give me up.

HENRY   You think I won't?

ALAIS   Because you told me so.

HENRY   You're not my Helen; I won't fight a war to save a face. We're done.

42

ALAIS   I don't believe you.

HENRY   Wait ten minutes.

GEOFFREY (*Entering*)   I've sent word to Durham. He'll be waiting in the chapel.

HENRY   Good—let's get it over with.

ALAIS   Don't do this to me, Henry.

HENRY (*To* RICHARD)   Take her.

ALAIS   No, wait. You don't want me, Richard.

HENRY (*To* ALAIS)   Go to him.

ALAIS (*As a procession forms around her*)   Not yet—(*To* PHILIP) I am your sister. Can't you find some pity for me? (*To* ELEANOR) *Maman*, you won't let this happen. (*Panic rising*) Henry, if you ever loved me—(*At a gesture from* HENRY, *the procession starts to move*) I won't do it. I won't say the words, not one of them. Henry, please. It makes no sense. Why give me up? What do you get? What are you gaining?

HENRY   Why, the Aquitaine, of course.

RICHARD (*Stopping dead*)   What's that?

HENRY   Your mother gets her freedom and I get the Aquitaine. (*To* ELEANOR) That is the proposition, isn't it? You did agree.

RICHARD (*To* ELEANOR)   Of course she did. I knew, I knew it. It was all pretense. You used me. God, and I believed you. I believed it all.

ELEANOR   I meant it all.

RICHARD   No wedding. There will be no wedding.

HENRY   But, my boy—

RICHARD   Not at this price.

HENRY   But Durham's waiting.

RICHARD   She's not worth the Aquitaine.

HENRY   You've simply got to marry her. It isn't much to ask. For my sake, Richard.

RICHARD   Never.

HENRY   But I've promised Philip. Think of my position.

RICHARD   Damn the wedding and to hell with your position.

HENRY   You don't dare defy me.

RICHARD   Don't I?

HENRY   (*To* PHILIP) You're the King of France, for goodness sake. Speak up. Do something.

RICHARD   (*To* PHILIP)   Make a threat, why don't you? Scare me.

PHILIP   Dunce.

RICHARD   Am I?

PHILIP   He never meant to have the wedding.

HENRY   Come again?

PHILIP   You're good at rage. I like the way you play it.

HENRY   Boy, don't ever call a king a liar to his face.

PHILIP   I'm not a boy. To you or anybody.

HENRY   Boy, you came here asking for a wedding or the Vexin back. By God, you don't get either one. It's no to both.

PHILIP   You have a pact with France.

HENRY   Then damn the document and damn the French. She'll never marry, not while I'm alive.

PHILIP   Your life and never are two different times.

HENRY   Not on my clock, boy.
(PHILIP *exits*)

RICHARD   Listen to the lion. Flash a yellow tooth and frighten me.

HENRY   Don't spoil it, Richard. Take it like a good sport.

RICHARD   How's your bad leg?

HENRY   Better, thank you.

RICHARD   And your back and all the rest of it. You're getting old. One day you'll have me once too often.

HENRY   When? I'm fifty now. My God, boy, I'm the oldest man I know. I've got a decade on the Pope. What's it to be? The broadsword when I'm eighty-five?

RICHARD   I'm not a second son. Not now. Your Henry's in the vault, you know.

HENRY   I know; I've seen him there.

RICHARD   I'll have the crown.

HENRY   You'll have what Daddy gives you.

RICHARD   I am next in line.

HENRY   To nothing.

RICHARD   Then we'll have the broadswords now.

HENRY   This minute?

RICHARD   On the battlefield.

HENRY   So we're at war.

RICHARD   Yes, we're at war. I have two thousand men at Poitiers.

HENRY   Can they hear you? Call and see who comes. You are as close to Poitiers as you're going to get.

RICHARD   You don't dare hold me prisoner.

HENRY   You're a king's son so I treat you with respect. You have the freedom of the castle.

RICHARD   You can't keep me here.

HENRY   Until we've all agreed that John comes next, I can and will.

RICHARD   The castle doesn't stand that holds me. Post your guards.
   (*He exits*)

JOHN   My God, I'm king again. Fantastic. It's a miracle. (*To* GEOFFREY, *who joins him*) Are you happy for me, Geoff?

GEOFFREY   (*As they exit together*)   I'm happy for us both.

ELEANOR   I came close, didn't I? (*To* ALAIS) I almost had my freedom and I almost had you for my son. I should have liked it, being free. (*To* HENRY) You played it nicely. You were good.

HENRY   I really was. I fooled you, didn't I? God, but I do love being king.

ELEANOR   Well, Henry, liege and lord, what happens now?

HENRY   I've no idea. I know I'm winning and I know I'll win but what the next move is—(*Looking at her closely*) You're not scared?

ELEANOR   No.

HENRY   I think you are.

ALAIS   I was. You musn't play with feelings, Henry; not with mine.

HENRY   It wasn't possible to lose you. I must hold you dearer than I thought. (*To* ELEANOR) You've got your enigmatic face on. What's your mood, I wonder.

ELEANOR   Pure delight. I'm locked up with my sons: what mother wouldn't dream of that? (*She moves to go, then stops in the doorway*) One thing.

HENRY   Yes?

ELEANOR   May I watch you kiss her?

HENRY   Can't you ever stop?

ELEANOR   I watch you every night. I conjure it before I sleep.

HENRY   Leave it at that.

ELEANOR   My curiosity is intellectual: I want to see how accurate I am.

HENRY   (*To* ALAIS) Forget the dragon in the doorway: come. (*Holding her*) Believe I love you, for I do. Believe I'm yours forever, for I am. Believe in my contentment and the joy you give me and believe—(*To* ELEANOR) You want more? (*Their eyes burn at each other. Then, turning slowly back to* ALAIS) I'm an old man in an empty place. Be with me.

   (*They kiss.* ELEANOR *stands in the doorway, watching*)

Dim and blackout

SCENE 5

ELEANOR's *chamber, shortly afterwards.* ELEANOR, *alone on stage, is seated at the table as the lights rise. A chest of jewels is on the table and she is feverishly covering herself with precious things.*

ELEANOR (*Putting on a great bib necklace*)   How beautiful you make me. What might Solomon have sung had he seen this? (*Picking up a mirror, unable to look*) I can't. I'd turn to salt. (*Putting the mirror down*) I've lost again. I'm done, for now. Well—there'll be other Christmases. (*Picking up another elaborate necklace*) I'd hang you from the nipples but you'd shock the children. (*Putting it on*) They kissed sweetly, didn't they? I'll have him next time. I can wait. (*Picking up a crown*) Ah, there you are; my comfort and my company. We're locked in for another year: four seasons more. Oh, what a desolation, what a life's work. (*Putting it on as* GEOFFREY *enters*) Is it too much? Be sure to squint as you approach. You may be blinded by my beauty.

GEOFFREY   Richard's raging all around the castle.

ELEANOR   Is he? Why?

GEOFFREY   He says it's got to do with being held a prisoner but I think he likes to rage.

ELEANOR   And John?

GEOFFREY John's skipping after Richard, saying naughty things.

ELEANOR And you?

GEOFFREY I thought you might be lonely.

ELEANOR (*Holding out the crown*) Here, Chancellor. Try it on for size.

GEOFFREY Why do you think so little of me?

ELEANOR Little? Never that. Whatever you are, you're not little.

GEOFFREY I remember my third birthday. Not just pictures of the garden or the gifts, but who did what to whom and how it felt. My memory reaches back that far and never once can I remember anything from you or Father warmer than indifference. Why is that?

ELEANOR I don't know.

GEOFFREY That was not an easy question for me and I don't deserve an easy answer.

ELEANOR There are times I think we loved none of our children.

GEOFFREY Still too easy, don't you think?

ELEANOR I'm weary and you want a simple answer and I haven't one. (*Starting to remove the jewelry*) I was thinking earlier of Peter Abélard. I was a queen of fifteen in those days and on dull afternoons I'd go watch Héloïse watch Abélard spread heresy like bonemeal in the palace gardens. Here the Seine and there the cypress trees and how it bored me. Thought, pure thought, flashed clear as water all around me and all I could think about was how to make a Caesar of a monkish husband. I'd like to hear the old man talk again; I'd listen now. For my ambition's thin with age and all the mysteries are as plump as ever. (*Looking at* GEOFFREY) I read minds. In yours, a shapely hand is writing, "Clever Mother, what's your clever reason for this clever talk?" It isn't clever but you'll make it so. (*Patting his cheek*) I am so sick of all of you.

JOHN (*Entering*)   I thought I'd come and gloat a little.

ELEANOR   Mother's tired. Come stick pins tomorrow morning; I'll be more responsive then.

JOHN   It's no fun goading anyone tonight.

ELEANOR   Come, let me look at you. I'm full of looks this evening. I have looked a little in the mirror and I've read a passage in your brother's mind; what's there to see in you? A little me, a little Henry and a lot of someone I don't know. (*Turning away*) Oh, John . . .

RICHARD (*Entering*)   The bastard's boxed us up.

ELEANOR   What's that, dear?

RICHARD   We're his prisoners, if that interests you.

ELEANOR   Why should it? I'm his prisoner anyway.

RICHARD   I've got to get to Poitiers. Henry wants a war, I'll give him one.

ELEANOR   I don't see how.

RICHARD   You seem to take that calmly.

ELEANOR   Well?

RICHARD   It was—correct me if I'm wrong, but it was my impression that you wanted Henry's throne for me.

ELEANOR   We've lost it this time, Richard. We can't win.

RICHARD   You think I'm finished, do you?

ELEANOR   So I do. I've suffered more defeats than you have teeth. I know one when it happens to me. Take your wormwood like a good boy. Swallow it and go to bed.

RICHARD   I will be king.

ELEANOR   And so you will. But not this year—and what's it matter to me anyway? The world stops when I die.

RICHARD   Yours does; mine doesn't.

ELEANOR   Leave it, Richard. Let it go for now. I have.

RICHARD   I can't.

JOHN   It's not so hard. Try saying after me: John wins, I lose.

RICHARD   What if John died?

JOHN   What's that?

RICHARD   What if he left us suddenly.

JOHN   You wouldn't dare.

RICHARD (*Going for his dagger*)   Why on earth wouldn't I?

JOHN   A knife—he's got a knife.

ELEANOR   Of course he has a knife. He always has a knife. We all have knives. It is eleven eighty-three and we're barbarians. How clear we make it. Oh, my piglets, we're the origins of war. Not history's forces nor the times nor justice nor the lack of it nor causes nor religions nor ideas nor kinds of government nor any other thing. We are the killers; we breed war. We carry it, like syphilis, inside. Dead bodies rot in field and stream because the living ones are rotten. For the love of God, can't we love one another just a little? That's how peace begins. We have so much to love each other for. We have such possibilities, my children; we could change the world.

GEOFFREY   And while we hugged each other, what would Philip do?

JOHN   Oh good God—Philip. We're supposed to start a war. If Father finds out, I'll be ruined.

GEOFFREY   Steady, John; don't panic.

JOHN Some advisor you are.

GEOFFREY Don't do anything without me. Let me handle it.

JOHN If you're so smart, why am I always doing something dumb?
(*He exits*)

ELEANOR (*Alive again*) Well, Geoffrey. He's made a pact with Philip. You advised John into making war. That peerless boy; he's disinherited himself. When Henry finds out, when I tell him what John's done—I need a little time. Can you keep John away from Philip till I say so?

GEOFFREY Anything you say.
(*He exits*)

ELEANOR (*To* RICHARD) I want you out of here before this breaks. And that needs Philip. He has soldiers with him if he'll use them. Go to him, be desperate, promise anything: the Vexin, Brittany. Then once you're free and John is out of favor, we'll make further plans.

RICHARD You talk to Philip. You're the diplomat; you see him.

ELEANOR You're a friend. You know him; I don't. Quickly now. (*He moves to exit*) And, Richard. (*He turns in the doorway*) Promise anything. (*He exits*) I haven't lost, it isn't over. Oh, I've got the old man this time. The damn fool thinks he loves John, he believes it. That's where the knife goes in. Knives, knives . . . it was a fine thought, wasn't it? Oh, Henry, we have done a big thing badly. (*Looking for her mirror*) Where's that mirror? I am Eleanor and I can look at anything. (*Gazing into the mirror*) My, what a lovely girl. How could her king have left her?

Dim and blackout

SCENE 6

PHILIP's *chamber, immediately following. It is a gracious room, its back wall lined with tapestries. A canopy bed, the curtains closed, stands at one side. A pair of chairs sit, one at each side of a low table on which there are two goblets and a wine decanter.*

As the lights rise, PHILIP *is preparing for bed. He turns as* GEOFFREY, *calling his name, comes skidding into the room.*

GEOFFREY   Philip, Philip—is John here?

PHILIP   Here? In my room?

GEOFFREY   Come on, Philip; this is me.

PHILIP   I've been expecting him.

GEOFFREY   The whole thing breaks tonight; we've reached the end of it.

PHILIP   If that's a warning, thank you.

GEOFFREY   What if it's an offer?

PHILIP   "What if" is a game for scholars: what if angels sat on pinheads?

GEOFFREY   What if I were king?

PHILIP   It's your game, Geoff; you play it.

GEOFFREY   All of England's land in France, from Normandy down to the Spanish border, once I'm king.

55

PHILIP   All that. What could I do that's worth all that?

GEOFFREY   By morning I can be the chosen son. The crown can come to me. But once it does, once Henry's favor falls my way, the war begins.

PHILIP   We have so many wars. Which one is this?

GEOFFREY   The one that Richard, John and Eleanor will make. I'll have to fight to keep what Henry, in his rage, is going to give me.

PHILIP   Yes, you will.

GEOFFREY   That's why I need you, Philip. Will you fight with me against them all?

PHILIP   Against them all?

GEOFFREY   Don't tell me it's a risk. I wouldn't hand you half of France to fight an easy war.

PHILIP   I wouldn't want you for an enemy.

GEOFFREY   Are we allies, then?

PHILIP   We were born to be.

GEOFFREY   I should say something solemn but I haven't time. I'm off to Father with the news that John's a traitor. After that—

JOHN (*Bursting from behind the tapestry*)   You stink, you know that? You're a stinker and you stink.

GEOFFREY   Come on. We're finished here.

JOHN   I'll kill you. Where's a dagger?

GEOFFREY   Hush, John, or you'll spoil everything.

JOHN   A sword, a spear, a candlestick. (*Reaching for a candlestick*) It's lights out, stinker.

GEOFFREY   (*Stopping him*) Dumb. If you're a prince, there's hope for every ape in Africa. I had you saved. I wasn't on my way to Father—but he was. He would have gone to Henry and betrayed you. Look: it's in his face.

JOHN (*Looking at* PHILIP *in dismay*)   Oh. It's true. I don't know who my friends are.

RICHARD (*Offstage, calling from a distance*)   Philip.

GEOFFREY (*Indicating the tapestry*)   May we?

PHILIP   That's what tapestries are for.

JOHN (*As* GEOFFREY *disappears, with him, behind the tapestry*)   I've ruined everything. I'll never learn.

PHILIP   Is someone there? I heard my name.

RICHARD (*Entering*)   I called it.

PHILIP   Richard. Hello, Richard.

RICHARD   You're halfway to bed. I'll wait for morning.

PHILIP   Come in.

RICHARD   Mother sent me.

PHILIP   Come in anyway. (*Filling glasses from the decanter*) Our alchemists have stumbled on the art of boiling burgundy. It turns to steam and when it cools we call it brandywine.

RICHARD   I'm Henry's prisoner.

PHILIP   So you said you'd go to war and Henry drew the drawbridge on you.

RICHARD   Do you find that charming?

PHILIP   No.

RICHARD   Then why the charming smile?

PHILIP   I thought, I can't think why, of when you were in Paris last. Can it be two whole years ago?

RICHARD   It can. I need an army, Philip.

PHILIP   (*Handing him the brandy*)   It will take the cold away.

RICHARD   I must have soldiers.

PHILIP   Have I aged? Do I seem older to you? They've been two fierce years: I've studied and I've trained to be a king.

RICHARD   I'll have your answer—yes or no.

PHILIP   (*Cold*)   You'll have it when I give it. (*Warm again*) See? I've changed. I'm not the boy you taught to hunt two years ago. Remember? Racing after boar, you flying first, me scrambling after, all day into dusk—

RICHARD   (*Turning to leave*)   I'll try another time.

PHILIP   Don't go.

RICHARD   I must know: will you help me?

PHILIP   Sit and we'll discuss it. (RICHARD *sits*) You never write.

RICHARD   To anyone.

PHILIP   Why should I make you King of England? Aren't I better off with John or Geoffrey? Why have you to fight when I could have the cretin or the fiend?

RICHARD   Would we fight?

PHILIP   We're fighting now. (*Terminating the interview*) Good night.

RICHARD   You're still a boy.

PHILIP   In some ways. Which way did you have in mind?

RICHARD   You haven't asked how much you're worth to me.

PHILIP   You'll tell me.

RICHARD   You can have the Vexin back.

PHILIP   And what else?

RICHARD   All of Brittany.

PHILIP   That's Geoffrey's.

RICHARD   Does that matter?

PHILIP   Possibly to Geoffrey. And what else?

RICHARD   That's all your help is worth.

PHILIP   And in return, what do you want from me?

RICHARD   Two thousand soldiers.

PHILIP   And what else?

RICHARD   Five hundred knights on horse.

PHILIP   And what else?

RICHARD   Arms and siege equipment.

PHILIP   And what else?

RICHARD   I never wrote because I thought you'd never answer. (PHILIP *says nothing*) You got married.

PHILIP   Does that make a difference?

RICHARD   Doesn't it?

PHILIP   I've spent two years on every street in hell.

RICHARD   That's odd: I didn't see you there. (PHILIP *takes* RICHARD's *hand. They start moving to the bed*) You haven't said you love me.

PHILIP   When the time comes.

HENRY (*Offstage, calling*)   Philip.

RICHARD   Don't go.

PHILIP   Hush.
         (*He opens the bed curtains*)

RICHARD Philip . . . (*Climbing through the curtains*) Hurry.

HENRY (*Still offstage*) Philip, lad.

PHILIP (*Closing the curtains*) Is someone there?

HENRY (*Entering*) I am. It's not too late at night?

PHILIP I've been expecting you.

HENRY Oh, have you?

PHILIP (*Indicating the glasses, his and* RICHARD'S) See— two glasses. I did hope you'd come.

HENRY Good; we can't leave negotiations where they are. I've seen more royal rooms. Poor Chinon wasn't meant to sleep so many kings. I keep looking for your father in you.

PHILIP (*Pouring brandy*) He's not there.

HENRY I miss him. Has Richard or the Queen been here to see you?

PHILIP Does it matter? If they haven't yet, they will.

HENRY I want to reach a settlement. I left you with too little earlier.

PHILIP Yes; nothing is too little.

HENRY I am sorry you're not fonder of me, lad. Your father always said, "Be fond of stronger men."

PHILIP No wonder he loved everyone.

HENRY They'll offer you whole provinces to fight me.

PHILIP Shocking. My advice to you is discipline your children.

HENRY I came here to offer peace.

PHILIP Piss on your peace.

HENRY Your father would have wept.

PHILIP   My father was a weeper.

HENRY   Fight me and you'll lose.

PHILIP   I can't lose, Henry. I have time. Just look at you.
Great heavy arms—they'd crush me like a leaf of lettuce.
But each year they get a little heavier. The sand goes pit-
pat in the glass. I'm in no hurry, Henry. I've got time.

HENRY   Suppose I hurry things along? What if I say that
England is at war with France?

PHILIP   Then France surrenders. I don't have to fight to
win. Take all you want—this county, that one. You won't
keep it long.

HENRY   What kind of courage have you got?

PHILIP   The tidal kind: it comes and goes.

HENRY   By God, I'd love to turn you loose on Eleanor.
More brandywine?

PHILIP   You recognize it?

HENRY   They were boiling it in Ireland before the snakes
left. Well, things look a little bleak for Henry, don't they?
You'll say yes to Richard when he comes; arms, soldiers,
anything he asks for.

PHILIP   I'd be foolish not to.

HENRY   And withdraw it all before the battle ever started.

PHILIP   Wouldn't you, in my place?

HENRY   Why fight Henry when his sons will do it for you?

PHILIP   Yes, exactly.

HENRY   You've got promise, lad. That's first-class thinking.

PHILIP   Thank you, sir.

HENRY   (*Emptying his glass*)   Good night.

PHILIP   (*Uncertain for the first time*)   Good night? You're going? (HENRY *nods benignly*) But we haven't settled anything.

HENRY We open Christmas packages at noon. Till then.

PHILIP You can't be finished with me.

HENRY But I am. And it's been very satisfactory.

PHILIP What's so satisfactory?

HENRY Winning is. I did just win. Surely you noticed.

PHILIP Not a thing. You haven't won a damn thing.

HENRY I've found out the way your mind works and the kind of man you are. I know your plans and expectations. You have burbled every bit of strategy you've got. I know exactly what you will do and exactly what you won't. And I've told you exactly nothing. To these aged eyes, boy, that's what winning looks like. *Dormez bien.*

PHILIP One time, when I was very small, I watched some soldiers take their dinner pig and truss it up and put the thing, alive and kicking, on the fire. That's the sound I'm going to hear from you.

HENRY And I thought you lacked passion.

PHILIP You—you made my father nothing. You were always better. You bullied him, you bellied with his wife, you beat him down in every war, you twisted every treaty, you played mock-the-monk and then you made him love you for it. I was there: his last words went to you.

HENRY He was a loving man and you learned nothing of it.

PHILIP I learned how much fathers live in sons. A king like you has policy prepared on everything. What's the official line on sodomy? How stands the Crown on boys who do with boys?

HENRY   Richard finds his way into so many legends. Let's hear yours and see how it compares.

PHILIP   He found me first when I was fifteen. We were hunting. It was nearly dark. I lost my way. My horse fell. I was thrown. I woke to Richard touching me. He asked me if I loved him—Philip, do you love me?—and I told him yes.

HENRY   I've heard much better.

PHILIP   You know why I told him yes? So one day I could tell you all about it. You cannot imagine what that yes cost. Or perhaps you can. Imagine snuggling to a chancred whore and, bending back your lips in something like a smile, saying, "Yes I love you and I find you beautiful." I don't know how I did it.

RICHARD (*Charging from the bed*)   No! It wasn't like that.

PHILIP   But it was.

RICHARD   You loved me.

PHILIP   Never.

RICHARD   Get your sword. You've got one. Pick it up.

PHILIP (*To* HENRY)   He's your responsibility; you talk to him.

RICHARD (*To* HENRY)   Get out. Please! I don't want you here.

HENRY   It's no great joy to be here.

RICHARD   So the royal corkscrew finds me twisted, does he?

HENRY   I'll go tell your mother: she'll be pleased.

RICHARD   She knows: she sent me.

HENRY   How completely hers you are.

RICHARD   You've had four sons. Who do you claim? Not

Henry? Not my buried brother. Not that monument to muck, that epic idiot, oh, surely not.

HENRY   The boy is dead.

RICHARD   Let's praise him, then. Who can forget his roquefort smile, his absent brow, those apey eyes, that spoon-edged mind? Why him? Why him and never me?

HENRY   He was the oldest. He came first.

RICHARD   Christ, Henry, is that all?

HENRY   You went with Eleanor.

RICHARD   You never called for me. You never said my name. I would have walked or crawled. I'd have done anything.

HENRY   It's not my fault. I won't be blamed.

RICHARD   I only wanted you.

HENRY   No—it's my crown. You want my kingdom.

RICHARD   Keep your kingdom.

HENRY   That I will.

RICHARD   I hope it kills you.

HENRY   I thank God I have another son. Thank God for John.

GEOFFREY   (*Stepping from behind the tapestry*)   Who shall we thank for Geoffrey? (*To* HENRY) You don't think much of me.

HENRY   Much? I don't think of you at all.

GEOFFREY   Nurse used to say I had your hands; I might have more of you. Try seeing me. I haven't Richard's military skill; but he was here betraying you, not I. I haven't John's I don't know what—God knows what you can see in John—and he's betrayed you, too. There's only me.

HENRY   You think I'd ever make you king?

GEOFFREY   You'll make me king because I'm all you've got. (*Indicating* RICHARD) I was to be his chancellor. Ask him why.

HENRY   I've heard enough.

GEOFFREY   For moving John to treason.

HENRY   I don't doubt he offered, I don't doubt you tried and I don't doubt John loves me.

GEOFFREY   Like a glutton loves his lunch.
     (*He pulls the tapestry from in front of* JOHN)

JOHN (*To* GEOFFREY)   You turd.

HENRY   Well, John?

JOHN   It isn't what you think.

HENRY   What do I think?

JOHN   What Geoffrey said. I wouldn't plot against you, ever.

HENRY   I know; you're a good boy.

JOHN   Can I go now, please? It's late. I ought to be in bed.

HENRY   You fool.

JOHN   Me? What have I done now?

HENRY   Couldn't you wait? Couldn't you trust me? It was all yours. Couldn't you believe that?

JOHN   Will you listen to the grief?

HENRY   Who do you think I built this kingdom for?

JOHN   Me? Daddy did it all for me? When can I have it, Daddy? Not until we bury you?

HENRY   You're just like them. And after all I've given you.

JOHN   I got it; I know what you gave.

HENRY   I loved you.

JOHN   You're a cold and bloody bastard, you are, and you don't love anything.

GEOFFREY   I'm it, I'm all that's left. Here, Father; here I am.

HENRY   My life, when it is written, will read better than it lived. Henry Fitz-Empress, first Plantagenet, a king at twenty-one, the ablest soldier of an able time. He led men well, he cared for justice when he could and ruled, for thirty years, a state as great as Charlemagne's. He married, out of love, a woman out of legend. Not in Alexandria or Rome or Camelot has there been such a queen. She bore him many children—but no sons. King Henry had no sons. He had three whiskered things but he disowned them. You're not mine. We're not connected. I deny you. None of you will get my crown. I leave you nothing and I wish you plague. May all your children breech and die. (*Moving unsteadily toward the door*) My boys are gone. I've lost my boys. (*Stopping, glaring up*) You dare to damn me, do you? Well, I damn you back. God damn you. All my boys are gone. I've lost my boys. Oh Jesus, all my boys.

Blackout and curtain

ACT TWO

SCENE 1

HENRY's *chamber, late at night. It is a large room, unadorned and without ornament. There is a plain hard bed, an armchair and a charcoal brazier. As the curtain rises,* ALAIS, *dressed for bed, is crouching by the brazier, adding spices to a pot of mulled wine.*

ALAIS (*Singing softly*)
The Christmas wine is in the pot,
The Christmas coals are red.
I'll spend the day
The lovers' way,
Unwrapping all my gifts in bed.
(ELEANOR *appears behind her*)
The Christmas goose is on the spit,
The Christmas . . .
(*She senses someone and turns*)

ELEANOR   No one else is caroling tonight. It might as well be Lent. When I was little, Christmas was a time of great confusion for me: the Holy Land had two kings, God and Uncle Raymond, and I never knew whose birthday we were celebrating.

ALAIS   Henry isn't here.

ELEANOR   Good; we can talk behind his back.

ALAIS   He's outside, walking.

ELEANOR   In this cold?

ALAIS He'll never notice it. What happened?

ELEANOR Don't you know?

ALAIS He came and stood awhile by the fire and went away. You would have liked the way he looked.

ELEANOR There was a scene with beds and tapestries and many things got said. Spiced wine; I'd forgotten Henry liked it. May I stay?

ALAIS It's your room just as much as mine: we're both in residence.

ELEANOR Packed in, like the poor, three to a bed.

ALAIS Did you love Henry—ever?

ELEANOR Ever? Back before the flood?

ALAIS As long ago as Rosamund.

ELEANOR Ah, that's pre-history, lamb; there are no written records or survivors.

ALAIS There are pictures. She was prettier than you.

ELEANOR Oh, much. Her eyes, in certain light, were violet and all her teeth were even. That's a rare fair feature, even teeth. She smiled to excess but she chewed with real distinction.

ALAIS And you hate her even now.

ELEANOR No, but I did. He put her in my place, you see, and that was very hard. Like you, she headed Henry's table; that's my chair.

ALAIS And so you had her poisoned.

ELEANOR That's a folk tale. Oh, I prayed for her to drop and sang a little when she did but even Circe had her limits. No, I never poisoned Rosamund. Why aren't you happy? Henry's keeping you. You must be cleverer than I am.

ALAIS   Green becomes you. You must always wear it.

ELEANOR   Are you dressing me in envy?

ALAIS   I've tried feeling pity for you but it keeps on turning into something else.

ELEANOR   Why pity?

ALAIS   You love Henry but you love his kingdom, too. You look at him and you see cities, acreage, coastline, taxes. All I see is Henry. Leave him to me, can't you?

ELEANOR   But I left him years ago.

ALAIS   You are untouchable. And I thought I could move you. Were you always like this? Years ago, when I was young and worshiped you, is this what you were like?

ELEANOR   Most likely. Child, I'm finished and I've come to give him anything he asks for.

ALAIS   Do you know what I should like for Christmas? I should like to see you suffer.

ELEANOR (*Nodding*)   Alais, just for you.

ALAIS (*Throwing herself into* ELEANOR's *arms*)   Maman, oh, Maman.

ELEANOR (*Singing softly*)
    The Christmas wine will make you warm—
    Don't shiver, child.

ALAIS   I'm not.

ELEANOR
    The Christmas logs will glow.
    There's Christmas cheer and comfort here—
    Is that you crying?

ALAIS   *Non, Maman.*

ELEANOR   Hold close and never let me go.
    (HENRY *appears behind them*)

HENRY   The sky is pocked with stars. What eyes the wise men must have had to spot a new one in so many.

ELEANOR   You look cold.

ALAIS   I've mulled some wine.

HENRY   I wonder, were there fewer stars then—I don't know. I fancy there's a mystery in it. (ALAIS *hands him a cup of wine*) What's this?

ALAIS   Warm wine.

HENRY   Why, so it is. (*Cupping her face in his hands*) You are as beautiful as I remembered. (*Briskly*) Off to bed. My widow wants to see me.

ALAIS   Let me stay.

HENRY   Wait up for me. I won't be long.

ALAIS   She came to find out what your plans are.

HENRY   I know that.

ALAIS   She wants you back.

HENRY (*To* ELEANOR)   Old as I am?

ELEANOR   Old as you are.

ALAIS   Oh, eat each other up for all I care. (*She starts to go, then stops and turns*) I'm an orphan and I'll never have a husband and my lover's wife has fangs for teeth and everybody's going to die. We've got no Romans and no Christians but the rest of the arena, that we have.
       (*She exits*)

ELEANOR   I'm rather proud; I taught her all the rhetoric she knows.

HENRY (*Pouring wine for her*)   So you want me back.

ELEANOR   She thinks I do. She thinks the need for loving never stops.

HENRY   She's got a point. I marvel at you: after all these years, still like a democratic drawbridge, going down for everybody.

ELEANOR   (*He gives her wine*)   At my age, there's not much traffic any more.

HENRY   To your interminable health. (*He drinks*) Well, wife, what's on your mind?

ELEANOR   Oh, Henry, we have made a mess of it.

HENRY   Yes, haven't we.

ELEANOR   Could we have done it worse?

HENRY   You look like Doomsday.

ELEANOR   Late nights do that to me. Am I puffy?

HENRY   Possibly: it's hard to tell; there's all that natural sag.

ELEANOR   I've just seen Richard.

HENRY   Splendid boy.

ELEANOR   He says you fought.

HENRY   We always do.

ELEANOR   It's his impression that you plan to disinherit them.

HENRY   I fancy I'll relent. Don't you?

ELEANOR   I don't much care. In fact, I wonder, Henry, if I care for anything. I wonder if I'm hungry out of habit and if all my lusts, like passions in a poem, aren't really recollections.

HENRY   I could listen to you lie for hours. So your lust is rusty. Gorgeous.

ELEANOR   I'm so tired, Henry.

73

HENRY Sleep, then. Sleep and dream of me with croutons. *Henri à la mode de Caen.*

ELEANOR Henry, stop it.

HENRY Eleanor, I haven't started.

ELEANOR What is it you want? You want the day? You've carried it. It's yours. I'm yours.

HENRY My what? You are my what?

ELEANOR Your anything at all. You want my name on paper? I'll sign anything. You want the Aquitaine for John? It's John's. It's his, it's yours, it's anybody's. Take it.

HENRY In exchange for what?

ELEANOR For nothing, for a little quiet, for an end to this, for God's sake sail me back to England, lock me up and lose the key and let me be alone. (HENRY *applauds, louder and louder*) You have my oath. I give my word. (*The applause stops. Sinking, bone-weary, into the chair*) Oh. Well. Well, well.

HENRY Would you like a pillow? Footstool? What about a shawl? (*She stares dully through him*) Your oaths are all profanities. Your word's a curse. Your name on paper is a waste of pulp. I'm vilifying you, for God's sake. Pay attention. (*No response*) Eleanor! (*She reaches out, takes his hand and kisses it*) Don't do that.
(*She drops the hand*)

ELEANOR (*Flatly, from far away*) Like any thinking person, I should like to think there was—I don't care whose or which—some God. Not out of fear: death is a lark; it's life that stings. But if there were some God, then I'd exist in his imagination, like Antigone in Sophocles'. I'd have no contradictions, no confusions, no waste parts or misplaced elements and then, oh, Henry, then I'd make some sense. I'd be a queen in Arcady and not an animal in

74

chaos. How, from where we started, did we ever reach this Christmas?

HENRY   Step by step.

ELEANOR   What happens to me now?

HENRY   That's lively curiosity from such a dead cat. If you want to know my plans, just ask me.

ELEANOR   Conquer China, sack the Vatican or take the veil; I'm not among the ones who give a damn. Just let me sign my lands to John and go to bed.

HENRY   No, you're too kind. I can't accept.

ELEANOR   Oh, come on, man. I'll sign the thing in blood or spit or bright blue ink. Let's have it done.

HENRY   Let's not. No, I don't think I want your signature on anything.

ELEANOR   You don't?

HENRY   Dear God, the pleasure I still get from goading you.

ELEANOR   You don't want John to have my provinces?

HENRY   Bull's eye.

ELEANOR   I can't bear you when you're smug.

HENRY   I know, I know.

ELEANOR   You don't want Richard and you don't want John.

HENRY   You've grasped it.

ELEANOR   All right, let me have it. Level me. What do you want?

HENRY   A new wife.

ELEANOR Oh.

HENRY Aesthete and poetaster that you are, you worship beauty and simplicity. I worship with you. Down with all that's ugly and complex, like frogs or pestilence or our relationship. I ask you, what's more beautiful and simple than a new wife?

ELEANOR So I'm to be annulled. Well, will the Pope annul me, do you think?

HENRY The Pontiff owes me one Pontificate; I think he will.

ELEANOR Out Eleanor, in Alais. Why?

HENRY Why? Not since Caesar, seeing Brutus with the bloody dagger in his hand, asked, "You, too?" has there been a dumber question.

ELEANOR I'll stand by it. Why?

HENRY A new wife, wife, will bear me sons.

ELEANOR That is the single thing of which I should have thought you had enough.

HENRY I want a son.

ELEANOR Whatever for? Why, we could populate a country town with country girls who've borne you sons. How many is it? Help me count the bastards.

HENRY All my sons are bastards.

ELEANOR You really mean to do it.

HENRY Lady love, with all my heart.

ELEANOR Your sons are part of you.

HENRY Like warts and goiters—and I'm having them removed.

ELEANOR   We made them. They're our boys.

HENRY   I know. And good God, look at them. Young Henry: vain, deceitful, weak and cowardly. The only patriotic thing he ever did was die.

ELEANOR   I thought you loved him most.

HENRY   I did. And Geoffrey: there's a masterpiece. He isn't flesh: he's a device; he's wheels and gears.

ELEANOR   Well, every family has one.

HENRY   But not four. Then Johnny. Was his latest treason your idea?

ELEANOR   John has so few ideas; no, I can't bring myself to claim it.

HENRY   I have caught him lying and I've said he's young. I've seen him cheating and I've thought he's just a boy. I've watched him steal and whore and whip his servants and he's not a child. He is the man we've made him.

ELEANOR   Don't share John with me; he's your accomplishment.

HENRY   And Richard's yours. How could you send him off to deal with Philip?

ELEANOR   I was tired. I was busy. They were friends.

HENRY   Eleanor, he was the best. The strongest, bravest, handsomest and from the cradle on you cradled him. I never had a chance.

ELEANOR   You never wanted one.

HENRY   How do you know? You took him. Separation from your husband you could bear. But not your boy.

ELEANOR   Whatever I have done, you made me do.

77

HENRY   You threw me out of bed for Richard.

ELEANOR   Not until you threw me out for Rosamund.

HENRY   It's not that simple. I won't have it be that simple.

ELEANOR   I adored you.

HENRY   Never.

ELEANOR   I still do.

HENRY   Of all the lies, that one is the most terrible.

ELEANOR   I know: that's why I saved it up for now. (*They throw themselves into each other's arms*) Oh, Henry, we have mangled everything we've touched.

HENRY   Deny us what you will, we have done that. And all for Rosamund.

ELEANOR   No, you were right: it is too simple. Life, if it's like anything at all, is like an avalanche. To blame the little ball of snow that starts it all, to say it is the cause, is just as true as it is meaningless.

HENRY   Do you remember when we met?

ELEANOR   Down to the hour and the color of your stockings.

HENRY   I could hardly see you for the sunlight.

ELEANOR   It was raining but no matter.

HENRY   There was very little talk as I recall it.

ELEANOR   Very little.

HENRY   I had never seen such beauty—and I walked right up and touched it. God, where did I find the gall to do that?

ELEANOR   In my eyes.

HENRY   I loved you.
   (*They kiss*)

ELEANOR   No annulment.

HENRY   What?

ELEANOR   There will be no annulment.

HENRY   Will there not?

ELEANOR   No; I'm afraid you'll have to do without.

HENRY   Well . . . it was just a whim.

ELEANOR   I'm so relieved. I didn't want to lose you.

HENRY   Out of curiosity, as intellectual to intellectual, how in the name of bleeding Jesus can you lose me? Do you ever see me? Am I ever with you? Ever near you? Am I ever anywhere but somewhere else?

ELEANOR   I'm not concerned about your geographical location.

HENRY   Do we write? Do I send messages? Do dinghies bearing gifts float up the Thames to you? Are you remembered?

ELEANOR   You are.

HENRY   You're no part of me. We do not touch at any point. How can you lose me?

ELEANOR   Can't you feel the chains?

HENRY   You know enough to know I can't be stopped.

ELEANOR   But I don't have to stop you; I have only to delay you. Every enemy you have has friends in Rome. We'll cost you time.

HENRY   What is this? I'm not moldering; my paint's not peeling off. I'm good for years.

79

ELEANOR How many years? Suppose I hold you back for one; I can—it's possible. Suppose your first son dies; ours did—it's possible. Suppose you're daughtered next; we were—that, too, is possible. How old is Daddy then? What kind of spindly, rickets-ridden, milky, semi-witted, wizened, dim-eyed, gammy-handed, limpy line of things will you beget?

HENRY It's sweet of you to care.

ELEANOR And when you die, which is regrettable but necessary, what will happen to frail Alais and her pruney prince? You can't think Richard's going to wait for your grotesque to grow?

HENRY You wouldn't let him do a thing like that?

ELEANOR Let him? I'd push him through the nursery door.

HENRY You're not that cruel.

ELEANOR Don't fret. We'll wait until you're dead to do it.

HENRY Eleanor, what do you want?

ELEANOR Just what you want: a king for a son. You can make more. I can't. You think I want to disappear? One son is all I've got and you can blot him out and call me cruel. For these ten years you've lived with everything I've lost and loved another woman through it all. And I'm cruel. I could peel you like a pear and God himself would call it justice. Nothing I could do to you is wanton; nothing is too much.

HENRY I will die sometime soon. One day I'll duck too slow and at Westminister, they'll sing out *Vivat Rex* for someone else. I beg you, let it be a son of mine.

ELEANOR I am not moved to tears.

HENRY I have no sons.

ELEANOR You've got too many sons. You don't need more.

HENRY   Well, wish me luck. I'm off.

ELEANOR   To Rome?

HENRY   That's where they keep the Pope.

ELEANOR   You don't dare go.

HENRY   Say that again at noon, you'll say it to my horse's ass. Lamb, I'll be rid of you by Easter: you can count your reign in days.

ELEANOR   You go to Rome, we'll rise against you.

HENRY   Who will?

ELEANOR   Richard, Geoffrey, John and Eleanor of Aquitaine.

HENRY   The day those stout hearts band together is the day that pigs get wings.

ELEANOR   There'll be pork in the treetops come the morning. Don't you see? You've given them a common cause: new sons. You leave the country and you've lost it.

HENRY   All of you at once.

ELEANOR   And Philip, too. He'd join us.

HENRY   Yes, he would.

ELEANOR   Now how's your trip to Rome?

HENRY   You'd truly do this to me?

ELEANOR   Oh, I've got you, got you, got you.

HENRY   Should I take a thousand men-at-arms to Rome or is that showy?

ELEANOR   Bluff away. I love it.

HENRY   Ah, poor thing. How can I break the news? You've just miscalculated.

ELEANOR Have I? How?

HENRY You should have lied to me. You should have promised to be good while I was gone. I would have let your three boys loose. They could have fought me then.

ELEANOR You wouldn't keep your sons locked up here?

HENRY Why the devil wouldn't I?

ELEANOR You don't dare.

HENRY Why not? What's to stop me? Let them sit in Chinon for a while.

ELEANOR No; I forbid it!

HENRY She forbids it!

ELEANOR Did your father sleep with me, or didn't he?

HENRY No doubt you're going to tell me that he did.

ELEANOR Would it upset you?

HENRY What about the thousand men? I say be gaudy and to hell with it.

ELEANOR Don't leave me, Henry. I'm at rock bottom, I'll do anything to keep you.

HENRY I think you think you mean it.

ELEANOR Ask for something.

HENRY Eleanor, we're past it; years past.

ELEANOR Test me. Name an act.

HENRY There isn't one.

ELEANOR About my fornication with your father—

HENRY Yes, there is. You can expire.

ELEANOR   You first, old man. I only hope I'm there to watch. You're so afraid of dying. You're so scared of it.

HENRY   Poor Eleanor; if only she had lied.

ELEANOR   She did. She said she never loved your father.

HENRY   I can always count on you.

ELEANOR   I've never touched you without thinking, "Geoffrey, Geoffrey."

HENRY   When you hurt me, I'll cry out.

ELEANOR   I've put more horns on you than Louis ever wore.

HENRY   Am I supposed to care?

ELEANOR   I'll kill you if you leave me.

HENRY   You can try.

ELEANOR   I loved your father's body. He was beautiful.

HENRY   It never happened.

ELEANOR   I can see his body now. Shall I describe it?

HENRY   Eleanor, I hope you die.

ELEANOR   His arms were rough, with scars here—

HENRY   Stop it!

ELEANOR   I can feel his arms. I feel them.

HENRY   AAH!

ELEANOR   What's that? Have I hurt you?

HENRY   Oh my God, I'm going to be sick.

ELEANOR   (*Hurling it after him as he exits*)   We did it. You were in the next room when he did it! (*He is gone. Bleakly, in desolation*) Well, what family doesn't have its

83

ups and downs? (*At the brazier, spreading her hands over it*) It's cold. I can't feel anything. (*Huddling close to the coals*) Not anything at all. (*Hugging herself, arms around tight*) We couldn't go back, could we, Henry?

Dim and blackout

SCENE 2

ALAIS'S *chamber, at dawn.* ALAIS, *dressed for bed as we saw her last, sits deeply asleep in a chair.* HENRY *enters, moves to the window, and throws back the curtain. His spirits are too high; the man is feverish and a little frightening.*

HENRY   Get up, wake up, it's morning.

ALAIS (*Startled*)   Henry?

HENRY   When the King is off his ass, nobody sleeps.

ALAIS   What's wrong?

HENRY   We're packing up and moving out.

ALAIS   Is there a war? What's happened?

HENRY   Merry Christmas.

ALAIS   Henry, what's the matter?

HENRY   Nothing, for a change; would you believe it?

ALAIS   Where've you been all night?

HENRY   You know what a *mesnie* is? It's a train, an entourage. It's made of soldiers, cooks and clerics, wagons, barrows, linen, treasure, chickens, butts of wine and spices. I've been all night making one.

ALAIS   What for?

HENRY   We're off to Rome to see the Pope.

ALAIS   He's excommunicated you again.

HENRY   He's going to set me free. I'm having Eleanor annulled. The nation will be shocked to learn our marriage
wasn't consummated.

ALAIS   What happened last night when I left?

HENRY   We hugged and kissed a little.

ALAIS   Oh, be serious.

HENRY   And then, I told her you and I were getting married.

ALAIS   Are we?

HENRY   By the Pope himself.

ALAIS   You mean it?

HENRY   Shall I kneel?

ALAIS   It's not another trick?

HENRY   The bridal party's drilling on the cobblestones.

ALAIS   She loves you, Henry.

HENRY   See for yourself.

ALAIS   She'll find a way to stop us.

HENRY   How? She won't be here. We're launching her for
Salisbury Tower when the winds change. She'll be barg-
ing down the River Vienne by lunchtime.

ALAIS   If she doesn't stop us, Richard will.

HENRY   Suppose I do the worrying.

ALAIS   He won't like losing me.

HENRY   He's lost a damn sight more than you. I've corked
him up.

ALAIS   You've what?

HENRY   He's in the cellar with his brothers and the wine.
The royal boys are aging with the royal port. You haven't
said "yes." Would you like a formal declaration? (*Kneeling, giving her his profile*) There—my finest angle; it's on
all the coins. Sad Alais, will you marry me?

ALAIS   I can't believe it.

HENRY   Be my Queen.

ALAIS   I never hoped for this. I mean, I always hoped but
never thought—I mean—

HENRY   We'll love each other and you'll give me sons.

ALAIS   I don't know what I mean.

HENRY   Let's have five; we'll do Eleanor one better. Why,
I'll even call the first one Louis if you like. Louis le Premier: how's that for a King of England?

ALAIS   Henry—you can't ever let them out.

HENRY   You've lost me. Let who out?

ALAIS   Your sons. You've put them in the dungeon and
you've got to keep them there forever.

HENRY   Do I now?

ALAIS   If they're free when you die, it's the dungeon or the
nunnery for me. I don't care which—a cell's a cell—but,
Henry, what about the child?

HENRY   Don't bother me about the child. The damn thing
isn't born yet.

ALAIS   If they're free, they'll kill it. I'm the one who'll live
to see that and I will not see our children murdered.

HENRY   You don't make the ultimatums: I do.

ALAIS Not this time. Either you keep them down forever or you find yourself another widow. I don't want the job.

HENRY Do you know what you're asking me to do?

ALAIS You locked your Queen up.

HENRY But my boys—how can I?

ALAIS That's for you to face.

HENRY You have no children.

ALAIS And I never will.

HENRY But they're my sons.

ALAIS I hate your sons. I'm not the one who wants a new line. If you want it, that's the price.

HENRY You'll come to Rome if I say so. You'll marry me if I say so. The boys go free if I say so. My terms are the only terms. The difficulty is, you see, the difficulty is you're right. (*So weary*) Incredible, but I have children who would murder children. Every time I've read *Medea*, I've thought: "No; the thing's absurd. Fish eat their young, and foxes: but not us." And yet she did it. I imagine she was mad; don't you? Yes, mad she must have been.
     (*He moves to go*)

ALAIS Henry—are you going down?

HENRY Down? Yes.

ALAIS To let them out or keep them in?

HENRY Could you say, to a child of yours, "You've seen the sunlight for the last time?"

ALAIS Can you do it, Henry?

HENRY Well, I'd be a master bastard if I did.

ALAIS I must know. Can you?

HENRY I shall have to, shan't I?
  (*He goes*)

> *Dim and blackout*

SCENE 3

The wine cellar, early morning. It is a large, dark and vaulted place; its walls and heavy door are offstage, lost in shadow. Candles flicker in tall candlesticks. There are great casks of wine and one small table in the cellar; nothing else.

RICHARD, JOHN and GEOFFREY are on stage as the lights rise. JOHN, at a cask of wine, is on the verge of replacing a bung with a spigot. RICHARD, holding two cups, stands by him. GEOFFREY stands apart.

JOHN   The trick is not to dribble when you bang the bung. (*He bangs it and slips the spigot into place*) Voilà. I had an alcoholic Latin tutor—cup (RICHARD *hands him a cup*) —who taught me all he knew.

GEOFFREY   Which wasn't much.

JOHN   I know I might as well be drunk.

GEOFFREY   If I were you, I'd worry.

JOHN   You know me—cup (*He gives* RICHARD *the full one and takes the empty*)—I'd just worry over all the wrong things.

GEOFFREY   Don't you know what's going to happen?

JOHN   No, and you don't either. You and your big cerebellum. (*Doing* GEOFFREY) "I'm what's left. Here, Daddy; here I am." And here you are.

RICHARD   But not for long.

GEOFFREY   You think we're getting out?

RICHARD   No; deeper in. The fortress at Vaudreuil has dungeons down two hundred feet. That's where I'd keep us.

GEOFFREY   And if I were Father, I'm not sure I'd keep the three of us at all. You don't take prisoners; no, you don't. And with good reason. Dungeon doors can swing both ways but caskets have no hinges.

JOHN   I know you. You only want to frighten me.

GEOFFREY   John, the condition of your trousers, be they wet or dry, could not concern me less. I think I'm apt to die today and I am sweating, John. I'm sweating cold.

JOHN   We've got friends.

GEOFFREY   Name one.

JOHN   Someone's got to rescue us.

GEOFFREY   I can't think who or how or why.

RICHARD   He isn't going to see me beg. He'll get no satisfaction out of me.

GEOFFREY   Why, you chivalric fool—as if the way one fell down mattered.

RICHARD   When the fall is all there is, it matters.

JOHN   Can't we run or hide or anything?

RICHARD   Just in the wine.

JOHN   (*Frightened by sounds of the cellar door opening*) Geoff—
    (ELEANOR *appears. She carries a large covered breakfast tray. Like Henry, she hasn't slept*)

ELEANOR   My barge is leaving at eleven and I've come to say good-bye.

GEOFFREY   Does Henry know you're here?

ELEANOR   The Queen still has some privileges. I bring you breakfast.

JOHN   I'm not hungry.

GEOFFREY   What's he planning?

RICHARD   Is he going to keep us here?

ELEANOR   First, have a little nourishment.

RICHARD   For God's sake, Mother—

ELEANOR   Eat.
   (*She drops the tray on the table. It makes a great metallic clatter.* RICHARD *removes the cover. The tray contains a stack of daggers and short swords*)

GEOFFREY   Well, Eleanor.

RICHARD   How heavy is the outside guard?

ELEANOR   There's just the turnkey.

RICHARD   What about the courtyard and the gates?

ELEANOR   They're putting Henry's train together and it's chaos. You can walk right out.

RICHARD   We'll go to Poitiers. He'll expect that but we'll meet him with an army when he comes. (*To* GEOFFREY *and* JOHN) Keep close to me and when you run, run hard.

GEOFFREY   Why run at all? I think we ought to stay.

JOHN   Stay here?

GEOFFREY   Till Henry comes. (*To* ELEANOR) He will come, won't he—and he'll come alone. (*To* RICHARD) I count three knives to one.

RICHARD   You think we could?

JOHN   I'd only do it wrong. You kill him and I'll watch.

GEOFFREY   The three of us together: we must all three do it. I want us all responsible.

ELEANOR   Don't listen to him. Take the knives and run.

GEOFFREY   And miss this opportunity?

ELEANOR   Get out.

GEOFFREY (*To* RICHARD)   I'll be behind the door with John. You'll want to do it from the front. (*To* ELEANOR) And you, you lucky girl, you get to see the pageant.

ELEANOR   Mother's looking for a name for you—if English has one adequately foul.

GEOFFREY   Now hold on. I've been vilified enough. I've had enough of it. You brought the cutlery, you hauled it down here. Don't you dare tell me this wasn't in your mind.

ELEANOR   I tell you. I deny it.

GEOFFREY   Swear on something. I'm agog to hear what you consider holy.
(*She turns abruptly and starts to go*)

RICHARD   Where are you going?

ELEANOR   Up for air.

GEOFFREY (*To* RICHARD, *who moves to intercept her*)   Don't stop her.

RICHARD   But she'll warn him.

GEOFFREY   Let her go. She isn't going to tell him anything.

ELEANOR   You think I'm going to let this happen?

GEOFFREY   Frankly, Mother, your position on the board is poorish. If you tattled, there would be a rash of executions and you don't want that. No, you don't want to lose a one of us: not even me.

ELEANOR   You're clever but I wonder if you're right.

GEOFFREY   Oh, lady, don't you know where you are? You're in stalemate. Warn him, it's the end of us: warn him not and it's the end of him. It's that clear.

ELEANOR (*Not very loud*)   Guard.

GEOFFREY   Go on, dear. Call again—and pitch it up a little.

ELEANOR   I'll have him take the knives away.

RICHARD   And be the one to put us in Vaudreuil, down two hundred feet?

ELEANOR   Then run away; escape. You've still got time.

RICHARD   No. Geoffrey's right; we'll stay.

ELEANOR   You, too? Oh, Richard.

RICHARD   Oh, oh, oh. There's nothing in your oh's: they're empty.

ELEANOR   You're not an assassin.

RICHARD   Look again.

ELEANOR   You're not. You're my Richard and you love me.

RICHARD   Let me kiss the nasty scratch and make it well.

ELEANOR   Yes, do. Come let me hold you.

RICHARD   You're more beautiful than ever. There is much that's beautiful in evil when it's absolutely pure. You are so foul you're fair. You stand there looking like a saint in pain when you brought us the knives to do your work.

ELEANOR   That's not true.

RICHARD   You did bring these things.

ELEANOR   Not for this.

RICHARD   Here—you want him dead, you do it.

ELEANOR   You unnatural animal.

RICHARD Unnatural, Mummy? You tell me, what's nature's way? If poisoned mushrooms grow and babies come with crooked backs, if goiters thrive and dogs go mad and wives kill husbands, what's unnatural? Here stands your lamb. Come cover him with kisses; he's all yours.

ELEANOR No, you're not mine. I'm not responsible.

RICHARD Where do you think I learned this from? Who do you think I studied under? How old was I when you fought with Henry first?

ELEANOR Young . . . I don't know.

RICHARD How many battles did I watch?

ELEANOR But those were battles, not a knife behind a door.

RICHARD I've never heard a corpse ask how it got so cold. You've got a mind: you tell me, what was on it when you had your soldiers point their crossbows at him?

ELEANOR That was in the field.

RICHARD I don't care if it's in the dahlia bed. What were you thinking, Eleanor?

ELEANOR Of you.

RICHARD Of your unnatural animal?

ELEANOR I did it all for you.

RICHARD You wanted Father dead.

ELEANOR No, never that.

RICHARD You tried to kill him, didn't you?

ELEANOR Yes.

RICHARD Why? What did you want?

ELEANOR I wanted Henry back.

RICHARD You lie.

ELEANOR I wanted Henry. Isn't there a chair?

JOHN (*Handing her his cup of wine*) Here. (*She takes it and reaches out to touch his cheek. He draws away*) None of that.

ELEANOR I've done without it this long; I'll endure.

GEOFFREY She'll warn him. I was wrong. She'll do it if she gets the chance.

ELEANOR Then you're in stalemate, aren't you, lamb?

GEOFFREY How so?

ELEANOR You don't dare let me stay here and you don't dare let me out. Dear me, whatever shall we do with Mother?

GEOFFREY Offhand there are several possibilities.

JOHN (*There are sounds of the door opening as he races to the table and slams the cover on the tray*) Watch it.
    (*HENRY appears, carrying an armful of huge candles. ALAIS follows*)

HENRY (*As he fills the empty candlesticks and ALAIS, with a taper, lights them*) It wants light. What we do in dungeons needs the shades of day. I stole the candles from the chapel. No one minded. Jesus won't begrudge them and the chaplain works for me.

ELEANOR You look dreadful.

HENRY So do you.

ELEANOR I underslept a little.

HENRY We can all rest in a little while. (*The candles are lit. The room is warm and cheery*) That's better. Bright and clear, just like the morning.

ELEANOR Here: I'll take the breakfast things.

RICHARD   Not yet.

ELEANOR   They've gotten cold.

RICHARD   They're good cold.

HENRY   Listen to me. What's the answer? Can I ever let you out?

RICHARD   What do you want from us? You must be mad. Why did you have to come here? Damn you, why'd you come?

HENRY   You think I want to lock you up?

RICHARD   You've got to. You can't let me out. You know you can't. I'll never stop.

HENRY   I can't stop either.

RICHARD   There's only fighting left.

HENRY   Not even that. What have you got to fight me with?

ELEANOR   (*As* RICHARD *and* GEOFFREY *start for the tray*)   My children. In the past, I've come and gone and loved you when it suited me. I never nursed you, warmed you, washed you, fed you, but today I felt such love for each of you and so I brought you breakfast.

RICHARD   Mother.

HENRY   Let her be.

ELEANOR   (*Removing the cover*)   I thought I had no other choice but I was wrong again.

HENRY   Brave boys; that's what I have. Three warriors. Who had first crack? How was I divided up? Christ—

RICHARD   You drove us to it.

HENRY   Don't stop now. You're killers, aren't you? I am. I

THE LION IN WINTER

can do it. (*To* GEOFFREY) Take a knife. (*To* RICHARD)
Come on. What is it? Come for me.

RICHARD   I can't.

HENRY   You're Richard, aren't you?

RICHARD   But you're Henry.

HENRY   Please. We can't stop and we can't go back. There's
nothing else.

JOHN   Daddy? Take me back. Please. Can't we try again?

HENRY   Again?

JOHN   We always have before.

HENRY   Oh yes . . . we always have.

JOHN   (*Running toward him, arms outstretched*) Oh,
Daddy—
   (*He comes skidding to a stop as* HENRY *draws his
   sword and holds it leveled at* JOHN's *vitals*)

ELEANOR   Go on. Execute them. You're the King. You've
judged. You've sentenced. You know how.

HENRY   By God, I will. Come Monday and they'll hang you
with the washing. There'll be princes swinging from the
Christmas trees.

ELEANOR   Why wait? They are assassins, aren't they? This
was treason, wasn't it? You gave them life—you take it.

HENRY   Who's to say it's monstrous? I'm the King. I call it
just. (*To his sons*) Therefore, I, Henry, by the Grace of
God King of the English, Lord of Scotland, Ireland and
Wales, Count of Anjou, Brittany, Poitou and Normandy,
Maine, Gascony and Aquitaine, do sentence you to death.
Done this Christmas Day in Chinon in God's year eleven
eighty-three. (*He moves to* RICHARD, *sword raised. He
swings the sword through the air and brings it crashing to*

the cellar floor. Into the silence he speaks, softly and thoughtfully) Surely that's not what I intended. Children . . . Children are . . . They're all we have. (*Spent, shattered, unable to look at anyone or anything, he waves them from the room*) Go on. I'm done, I'm done. I'm finished with you. Never come again.

(JOHN, GEOFFREY *and* RICHARD *exit*)

ELEANOR You spare the rod, you'll spoil those boys.

HENRY I couldn't do it, Eleanor.

ELEANOR Nobody thought you could.

HENRY I did.

ALAIS You saved them. You maneuvered it.

ELEANOR Did I?

ALAIS They're free because of you. They'll kill him one day; you know that.

ELEANOR The next time or the next.

ALAIS You always win, *Maman.*

ELEANOR Except the prize.

ALAIS (*To* HENRY) Come rest.

HENRY I want no women in my life.

ALAIS You're tired.

HENRY I could have conquered Europe, all of it, but I had women in my life.

ALAIS I'll warm some wine.

HENRY I've shot your world, you silly bitch, and there you stand, all honey and molasses. Sweet? You make my teeth ache.

(*They embrace*)

ELEANOR   That's touching. Is it for my benefit?

HENRY   Your benefit? (*To* ALAIS) Get out. Go on. Go.

ALAIS   When you want me, I'll be waiting.
(*She exits*)

HENRY (*Turning on* ELEANOR)   For your benefit? I've done enough on your account. I should have killed you years ago.

ELEANOR   There's no one peeking. Do it now.

HENRY   I've wasted fortunes, squandered lives, spent everything—to buy this pit. I've got an eye for value. This is what I've made. I meant to do so much.

ELEANOR   Is this a play for pity?

HENRY   Not from you. You put me here. You made me do mad things. You've bled me.

ELEANOR   Shoulder it yourself. Don't put it on my back. You've done what you have done and no one but yourself has made you do it. Pick it up and carry it. I can. My losses are my work.

HENRY   What losses? I've been cheated, not you. I'm the one with nothing.

ELEANOR   Lost your life's work, have you? Provinces are nothing: land is dirt. I've lost you. I can't ever have you back again. You haven't suffered. I could take defeats like yours and laugh. I've done it. If you're broken, it's because you're brittle. You are all that I have ever loved. Christ, you don't know what nothing is. I want to die.

HENRY   You don't.

ELEANOR   I want to die.

HENRY   I'll hold you.

ELEANOR I want to die.

HENRY Stop saying that. Let me do something, damn you. This is terrible.

ELEANOR Henry, I want to die.

HENRY You will, you know. Wait long enough and it'll happen.

ELEANOR (*Smiling*) So it will.

HENRY We're in the cellar and you're going back to prison and my life is wasted and we've lost each other and you're smiling.

ELEANOR It's the way I register despair. There's everything in life but hope.

HENRY We have each other and for all I know that's what hope is.

ELEANOR We're jungle creatures, Henry, and the dark is all around us. See them? In the corners, you can see the eyes.

HENRY And they can see ours. I'm a match for anything. Aren't you?

ELEANOR I should have been a great fool not to love you.

HENRY Come along; I'll see you to your ship.

ELEANOR So soon?

HENRY There's always Easter Court.

ELEANOR You'll let me out for Easter?

HENRY Come the resurrection, you can strike me down again.

ELEANOR Perhaps I'll do it next time.

HENRY And perhaps you won't.

ELEANOR (*Taking his arm, moving to go*) It must be late
and I don't want to miss the tide.

HENRY (*As they go*) You know, I hope we never die.

ELEANOR I hope so, too.

HENRY You think there's any chance of it?

Curtain

ϕ - 3/08